Walking in
Historic Yorkshire

by

Colin Speakman

THE DALESMAN PUBLISHING COMPANY LTD.,
CLAPHAM (via Lancaster).
YORKSHIRE.

First Published 1971

© Colin Speakman, 1971.

Printed and bound in Great Britain by
FRETWELL & BRIAN LTD.
Silsden, Nr. Keighley, Yorkshire.

12 msc

N67787

40p.

By the same author:
THE DALES WAY
TRANSPORT IN YORKSHIRE

Other "Dalesman" books for the walker:
LYKE WAKE WALK
THE PENNINE WAY
WALKING IN DERBYSHIRE

Contents

The front cover illustration shows a stretch of typical Yorkshire walking country in Widdale.

The map on the back cover is by Janet Acland and maps in the text by E. Gower.   Title page photograph by David Joy shows the Bridestones (Walk No. 1).

Introduction

WHEN *Dalesman* asked me to revise *Walking in the York-shire Dales* for republication, it seemed to me that successful as the book had been, it was now no longer fulfilling quite the need it once had. Imitation is the best form of flattery, and since that *Dalesman* book several Dales guides have appeared, some indeed covering the very same paths. Moreover, reports from readers have convinced me that the most popular walks in the book were the shorter, circular walks for the motorised walker, and since the withdrawal of several bus and rail services in the National Park some walks in the older book are now, alas, physically impossible to do without two cars and two drivers. A complete revision was therefore necessary. I was also becoming increasingly aware of the enormous interest in the Yorkshire countryside not merely as a pretty backcloth to pleasant exercise, but as a living document of human history. An upsurge of interest in the environment, and in particular the human dimensions in the environment, archaeology, its more recent cousin industrial archaeology, architecture, and in the evidence of the very landscape itself, led me to attempt a sort of "History of Yorkshire from the Footpath."

For footpaths provide a unique means of penetration into a landscape—a closeness, an intimacy with the environment free of the barriers that any means of mechanical transport-ation must impose. We have on foot time to observe, to explore, to see the old and even the familiar from unusual perspectives. Indeed actual means of transportation, from foot, horse and waggon to barge, locomotive and car, have all left their distinct mark on our landscape heritage, and the rambler is in a most excellent position to discover and even re-use these older ways. Moreover all human habitation exists in the con-text of a wider landscape and is shaped by enormous geological and human forces. To approach a building, a monument, a village or even a town on foot is to have a splendid opportunity to observe these forces—if one can only interpret the evidence.

Landscape is not created by nature alone, but by generations of men shaping and forming their environment, sometimes achieving a fine harmony, as in a beautiful garden, parkland, or rich, well cared-for rural landscape; perhaps dominating or even destroying nature, as in an urban or industrial land-scape, or, as many believe, in our new factory or "prairie" farms; or perhaps, most-thought provoking of all, being defeated by nature, as on upland farms reverting to wilderness, or mine workings being reclaimed by grass or woodland. This little book explores all these things.

It is rapidly being realised that history and geography have little meaning for young people when purely confined to textbooks. New techniques of "environmental studies" being developed in more progressive schools and colleges attempt to unravel the forces at work in a landscape and to illustrate what was once understood as "pure" history or geography. This book will I hope be especially valuable to teachers and students in these disciplines, as well as the more casual rambler. I have attempted therefore to organise my walks chronologically, and select rambles in which a characteristic type of landscape or feature, be it village, castle or mere foot-path, seems to be dominant on at least one part of the walk.

Yorkshire is, of course, immensley rich in historical material and landscape of the highest quality, and my difficulty has been to exclude material rather than include. I have chosen to put the emphasis on providing a fine walk rather than perhaps choosing a major historical feature—Almondbury, The Devil's Arrows and Marston Moor would be three examples of immensely important historical sites which I have rejected because I have failed to find an adequate walk in which to set them. But other features, notably Fountains, Grass Wood or Castle Howard, provide no such dilemma for each exists in a superb setting. Almost throughout I have made walks circular, to and from the inevitable parked car, but I have also only chosen walks which—at least at time of writing—can be reached by public transport. Country towns have been in-cluded but I have avoided cities, partially because of their complexity (York, a city of European significance, demands a book to itself) and partially because the most fascinating and atmospheric parts of our great Victorian cities, Leeds, Brad-ford and Sheffield, are likely to suffer demolition hammers in the near future.

Naturally each "period" landscape only contains elements of that period frozen by accident or good fortune amid later developments. Indeed readers may very well feel that another

7

age is equally present on a walk—the best packhorse bridges appear on a Victorian walk and the most authentic Bronze Age track is in a "Roman" section. So be it. A writer has the privilege of a personal choice, and if as a result of this little book you discover better examples, that will be adequate tribute to its success.

I began in pre-history, among the relics of the Urn people on Blackamoor, and was able to find enough of the Iron Age Brigantes and Romano-British peoples to suggest some exciting walks. The Saxons were more elusive, for although villages and fieldpaths might date from Anglian times, much has altered. The Middle Ages were easier; castles and monasteries and, packhorse ways still abound, and likewise it was a pleasure to select typical eighteenth century villages, parkland and early industrialism. It was perhaps a little sad to end the book with the Victorians—an early Victorian town and a later Victorian railway. On reflection this might be because so much typically twentieth century landscape is on such a vast scale that you can't really enjoy it on foot—a motorway (it would have been nice to include a bit of the M62 which is visually very exciting) or new industrial estate are not for the pedestrian. But to be really honest, so much typically twentieth century development is downright dull and ugly and somehow seems to blunt the human spirit—the pylons, the industrial deserts, the uniformity of suburbia. Enough of this will intrude anyhow, without having to seek it out. Even Niklaus Pevsner, who enthuses about many of Yorkshire's great and small buildings, finds very little built after 1880 worth more than a couple of lines. It might be merely the golden haze that time gives to everything (even the splendours of Victorian architecture were sneered at a decade ago) but this thought cannot erase the nagging certainty that with rare exceptions our own era has turned much of our unique landscape to a vast featureless desert. I have tried to conceive of a walk, however short, that was both beautiful and yet typical of our own age. The fact that I was unable to do so, I find seriously disquieting.

There are slightly less walks in this book, simply because I wanted to devote more space to history and a fuller description. Even so, I have felt the need to include further reading at the end of most walks to enable the reader to develop his awareness a little more fully. Three walks will be recognised as familiar of *Walking in the Yorkshire Dales*. This isn't just poverty of imagination; I happen to consider them the most impressive and best solution to that particular problem and

Walking in historic Yorkshire. A party of ramblers head on to the edge of Osmotherley moor. (Roy Shaw)

to be worth revising. I have tried to give variety of terrain and distance, and have been able to choose routes of between four and 14 miles from all three Ridings. I regret only being able to use one walk from the East Riding's beautiful and historic Wolds—this is not from choice, but because in that county pressure from landowners and farmers has succeeded in eliminating so many footpaths over the years, that the walks I would have liked to include are just not legally possible. This is a selfish and a short-sighted attitude and it may take years before the position is rectified and rights-of-way restored.

In a book of limited size and ambitious scope, directions are inevitably subject to compression and ambiguity of language. I have attempted to reduce this, but I must insist that words are no replacement for maps, and a large scale map of at least one inch scale and preferably $2\frac{1}{2}$ inch must be carried. I give grid references where difficulty either might be expected, or a point is not immediately clear on the map. There is no substitute for good map-reading—use the book sketch maps merely to supplement and not replace the Ordnance Map. Intelligently used, the book should help develop the art of map reading and footpath finding, which is a valuable craft.

9

Even then it would be remarkable if at some time you didn't miss a path. I have gone to some trouble to avoid really difficult paths, and most are very easy to follow, but the odd one that is tricky has remained in, rather than ruin an entire walk. Local people are with very rare exceptions most helpful and indeed grateful for the company of a well-intentioned visitor.

Although almost every path suggested in this book is a public right of way or well established "permissive" route, this does not give you authority to disregard the needs and feelings of those who live on the land. Remember you are a rare visitor, but they are there for the other 364 days of the year. Always remember and obey the Country Code, and at all costs keep dogs on leads and avoid leaving gates open, dropping litter or damaging walls. Almost every path I surveyed in compiling this book was clear at the time of writing, but should you discover an obstruction such as barbed wire, fallen stile or fierce bull make an exact note of the place, giving a grid reference, and submit a written report to the Highways Department, County Hall, Beverley, Wakefield or Northallerton for East, West or North Riding respectively. Paths in arable areas suffer most, walks 2, 6, 11, 14, 17 and 18 being most at risk. Where paths are ploughed, legally you should walk directly on line of the path across the ploughing or crop, though most people will prefer to detour round the edge of the field.

Mud on footpaths is the price of a good walk, especially after wet weather or in winter. Light boots are strongly recommended—both for supporting ankles on steep hillsides and to keep feet dry on soft ground. To lose a shoe in marshy ground is no joke. Walks 1, 4, 5, 7, 8, 11, 15, 17, 18, 20 and 21 are most suitable for school parties, using public transport or coaches, but teachers should know the capacity of their charges as walkers, see that they are properly dressed and shod, and keep them well behaved in the countryside. Country folk don't value a horde of rowdy urchins or teenagers in their farm or village.

Finally, I must record my gratitude to East Riding Ramblers for information about paths round Flamborough, to Craven‧ Group of the Ramblers for waymarking paths through Grass Wood, and to Mr. Bob Brewster of Tadcaster for some most helpful survey material around Towton. And, of course, to all those members of the Ramblers' Association and local footpath groups who are so enthusiastically guarding our footpath heritage to make little books of this nature possible.

1: *The Bronze Age*

Bridestones and Blakey Topping—8 miles.

THE North York Moors, more than anywhere else in the North of England, retain something of a feeling and a flavour of Bronze Age times—a vast, primeval, brooding quality and a primitive magic. According to Elgee this is perhaps because the Urn people who retreated to the lonely and desolate heights of Blackamoor when fresh invaders captured these islands, remained undisturbed perhaps right into historic times. This short but dramatic walk tries to convey something of this atmosphere. The village of Lockton is the starting point, easily reached just off the Pickering-Whitby road by car or United bus from Malton. Motorists will find room to park on the verge of the lane leaving the north of Lockton (SE 846899). Walk to the main Pickering-Whitby road, crossing to the centre gate opposite just to the right of the signpost and entering a pretty green lane that drops into the wooded valley of Green Dale. It soon climbs up through forestry land to join a farm track from Thwaite Head (858899). A right-of-way branches off this track to behind Pasture House, but as it is in an extremely poor condition, it is advisable to continue along to the junction of tracks (863903) turning right to Pasture House.

Now go straight ahead past the farm, descending down a delectable green track curving left (ignore stile in corner) to Low Staindale. Until recently this was one of the remotest and most attractive of Youth Hostels, but now it is unfortunately closed. Staindale is a beautiful valley, enclosed by dense Forestry Commission plantations which may be rather ugly in themselves, but shelter the valley bottom. Continue past the old hostel, descending to the stream and then climbing up to a small gate, above and to the left. This is the entrance to the Yorkshire Naturalists Trust's Bridestones Nature Reserve which is also a National Trust property—take extra care here to avoid damaging plant life. Follow the path climbing steeply right. Soon Bridestones come into view— massive outcrops of Corallian limestone, weathered into

11

fantastic shapes like huge monoliths. The name "Bride" implies association with "Bridget" or "Brigid," the old Bronze-age Pagan fire goddess and is clearly a relic of local superstition.

Explore the great stones perched precariously over the valley. After the last of these do not descend, but retrace your steps past the last two rocks and look for a narrow path branching off behind them (873915). This needs care to find, but you should soon be making your way to the dark forestry plantation on your right and a broad track. Follow this right to the end of Grime Moor (866934), turning right at the cross roads down a concreted track to Newgate Foot Farm, an attractive little settlement. It is close to Blakey Topping, the mysterious conical hill in the foreground which is a result of freak erosion, leaving the peak of hard sandstone like a gigantic man-made structure. Behind, on Fylingdales Moor, the strange spherical structures of the Early Warning Station make a startling contrast—a clash of two cultures, Bronze Age and Technological.

Descend straight through the farm, and as the track below rises through an open gateway cut right across the rough pasture to reach an "elbow" in the track ahead (873934). Here is Blakey Topping Circle, a Bronze Age monument erected between 1,600 and 1,000 B.C. Not all the stones remain, and the circle's purpose will perhaps remain ever obscure, but the dominant and overpowering form of Blakey Topping behind together with the natural amphitheatre in the hills suggests a powerful religious significance. A mile due south-west on Thompson's Rigg are numerous Bronze Age tumuli, clearly relating to the circle in some way. Retrace your steps but before the farm branch right at two asbestos-roofed barns and go along a faint track. This reaches a gate, and enters a green way by a young forestry plantation. Follow it slightly left (866942) through more gates until it becomes a stony forestry track climbing to Malo Cross at the end of Whinny Nab (867949)

Malo Cross is one of those ancient Cleveland crosses, so frequently found at road junctions, which are full of pre-Christian associations. Many date back to Anglian times and some even earlier. Don't go through the gate, but keep to the south side of the fence along an ancient way (possibly a branch of the packhorse road from Robin Hood's Bay, or perhaps actually a Bronze Age route) which climbs the side of Whinny Nab. It gives superb views of the surrounding moorland, soon crossing the line of an ancient dyke that perhaps

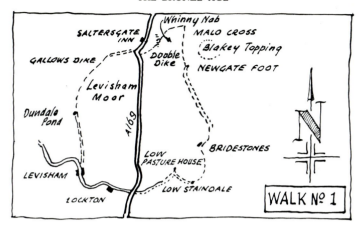

made this hill the fortified homestead of some tough old hill tribe. The track broadens out of the bilberries by the edge of arable fields, with the white *Saltergate Inn,* the famous Cleveland hostelry on the Salter's route to Whitby, on the main road below. Go through a white gate, bearing left to a second gate in the field corner, to reach the A109. Cross the road, walking round the lip of the Hole of Horcum, a vast natural basin in the moorland. At the sharp bend in the road, by another ancient earthwork at Gallows Dike (847941), take the sandy track which curves through the heather along the moortop giving exciting views over Levisham Moor. This is an area pockmarked with ancient earthworks and barrows, while the dramatic gorge of Newton Dale is over to your right, with George Stephenson's Whitby-Pickering railway snaking through it. At Dundale Pond (829919), keep slightly left to reach a broad green lane that drops down to Levisham village. Descend the steep hairpin bend climbing back up to Lockton and your car or bus.

Maps: One Inch Sheet 92 or North York Moors Tourist.
Sources: Ian Longworth: "Regional Archaeologies - Yorkshire"
(1965).
Frank Elgee: "Early Man in North East Yorkshire"
(1930).

The Iron Age

Danes Dyke and Flamborough Head—2 to 14 miles.

ONE of the most dramatic and curious corners of Yorkshire is where that massive chalk headland juts out into
the North Sea at Flamborough Head. The little peninsula is
divided from the "mainland" by a deep-man-made ravine,
"Danes Dyke." In spite of its name it undoubtedly dates from
Iron Age times, and probably from between 300 B.C. and
100 A.D. when Celtic peoples—in this area the Parisii—
formed loose federations of tribes. It needs little imagination
to see Flamborough as a defensive tribal settlement, bounded
on three sides by sea and on the fourth by earthworks of
gigantic proportions.

This walk explores much of this little kingdom, and is
notable for spectacular cliff scenery. You can start from
Bridlington walking along the promenade, then the clifftop
to Sewerby (a Georgian House with fine gardens), and continuing to the Danes Dyke nature trail. Motorists might
prefer to start at Danes Dyke itself, turning off the Flamborough road at the large blue entrance sign. At the instigation
of the East Riding Ramblers' Association during Conservation
Year 1970, Bridlington Corporation has made an admirable
job of clearing paths and making steps and footbridges for the
benefit of visitors. Walkers from Bridlington turn left above
the Dyke at the clifftop, soon entering the path above the
wood. Ignore a stile that appears on the left, and keep left
with the Nature Trail sign where the path dips away right.
This goes along the ravine opposite the Dyke, giving the
walker a chance to see its massive proportions. It would, of
course, have been even higher when in use, probably with a
wooden stockade to make it virtually impregnable. Motorists
from the car park will have joined this path by turning left
along the wall just above the park, and then climbing up steps
and going right at the top.

The path finally crosses a footbridge and enters the estate
drive. Go right along the drive built into the middle of the
Dyke, but then take the lane to the left that goes through a

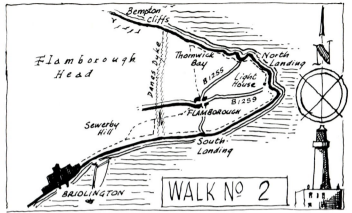

breach in the Dyke (216696) past Dyke Cottages. Where it bends left take the path commencing at an iron fence post and going between hedge and fence. This follows the fence to the left, making for Flamborough's squat twelfth century church ahead. The village of Flamborough might have been the site of an original Iron Age settlement, though the modern bungalows are anything but Celtic. Go right at the lane to the church along the main road, but left at the cross roads towards North Landing. Pass the ruins of the castle in the field on your left and several fishing cottages and inns, more characteristic of the East Riding. A granite memorial recalls the ever-present hostility of the sea.

Towards the end of the village, where the roads bend slightly right with open country on your left, follow the path that should still be marked by an elderly wooden sign to Bempton and Cliff top (226708). This soon turns right alongside a fence and at a second sign, indicating the clifftop, take the path to the left of a hedge. The farmer tends to plough to the very edge of the field, so keep close to the hedge. Remains of stiles mark the way, which bears left behind a huge caravan site and crosses gorsey grassland before finally reaching the clifftop at a good stile.

Turn right along the clifftop. The path is quite visible on the ground, with spectacular views of cliff and foreshore along what is a nationally famous bird sanctuary. Remember that the cliffs are dangerous and prone to landslides, so maintain a safe distance and keep children under control. But the views across the sea, the sense of space and of light, particularly if sunlight is on the water, make this walk quite unforgettable.

15

Just past Thornwick Nab there is a small cafe with a red roof—go between it and the sea keeping in the same direction to a tarmac road. Once round the indentation of the cliff, keep between the clifftop bungalows and the sea, working round a long ravine to the North Landing lifeboat station. The paths here aren't maintained as they might, as their legality is still undecided. But from the lifeboat station onwards the path is good and clear, coming round by the ever more dramatic cliffs to the Head itself. The sculptured shapes of the cliffs, with huge arches and free-standing stacks, are particularly impressive, and the chalky soil sustains wide varieties of wild flowers in the late spring months.

The little gate to the left of the lighthouse indicates the path, keeping to the shore side of the siren station and making for the dramatic cliff edge again. The path from here onwards is less well used—stiles sometimes are a trifle wobbly, and you must sometimes tread carefully between ploughed land and the field edge, and occasionally drop down a steep ravine. Such a one is South Landing, a natural little harbour and delightful beach but a ravine to be descended with care. It seems probable that such a place must once have been fortified, although constant erosion has doubtless cut much of the coastline and evidence away. The path now climbs over Beacon Hill and finally reaches Danes Dyke again. Turn right along the nature-trail path on the crest of the Dyke, which eventually joins the main drive. Turn right again up to the car park.

Walkers returning to Bridlington should turn left at the top of the car park, along the wall, down the footbridge and up the steps straight ahead to the stile in the hedge by a signpost. This is a pleasant path, first through farmland and then through parkland back to Sewerby and Bridlington. To and from Bridlington the walk is about 14 miles, but about three shorter from Danes Dyke car park. There is moreover a regular bus service from Flamborough village back to Bridlington (consult the East Yorkshire timetable), which will enable this walk to be easily shortened from several points.

Maps: One Inch Sheet 93; 2½ Inch sheet TA27.
Sources: Thomas Shepherd: "Geological Rambles in East Yorkshire" (1903).
Fairfax - Blakeborough: "Yorkshire - East Riding" (1951).
National Parks Commission: "The Coasts of Yorkshire and Lincolnshire" (HMSO 1968).

3:   *The Iron Age*

Ingleborough Hill Fort—11 miles.

CARTIMANDUA was Queen of the Brigantes, the federation of Iron-age tribes that lived in what is now West Yorkshire. She betrayed her country to the Romans and deserted her husband Venutius for a favourite servant. Venutius led a ferocious rearguard action from the Pennine hills before final defeat at Stanwick, one of the most spectacular of his strongholds being Ingleborough.

Begin from Clapham, bearing left at the top of the village and either entering the Ingleborough estate by paying a small fee at the cottage on the right (a pretty woodland walk) or taking the public bridle path entered by the gate a few yards further up on the right. This latter climbs up above the estate woodland, but turn right at the small building at Clapdale to return to the valley track below Ingleborough cave and the spectacular dry gorge of Trow Gill. Follow the wall on the left above Trow Gill to cross the stone step stile leading to the broad moorland path and the celebrated cave entrance of Gaping Gill (SD 752727)—it is possible to make a descent of this enormous cavern on most bank holidays when the caving clubs operate their winch. Continue up the well-used track up the edge of Little Ingleborough and on to the shoulder plateau of the mountain and the final great summit block.

As you scramble up the last few yards to the high plateau note the loose stones—remains of the Brigantian wall that surrounded the fort. On the flat summit the outlines of the hut circles of the encampment are still clearly visible. The summit cairn and wind shelter are the remains of a nineteenth century tower, probably built from the ancient fort remains. The views are of course superb in all directions; this is unquestionably one of the finest mountains in England.

Make your way off the summit heading northwestwards along the ridge between Ingleborough and Simon Fell. Do not however climb Simon Fell, but bear right keeping your height along Simon Fell Breast, with fine views down Clapdale towards the Bowland Fells. You will soon reach a ladder stile

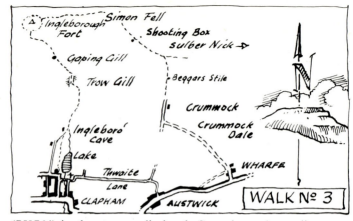

(758764) in the stone wall ahead. Cross here, descending now but going through the wall on your left at a convenient gap to pass an old shooting hut (767740) and cross fine limestone pavements by Nick Pot and Sulber Pot. You are now walking along one of the iron age routes up Ingleborough, doubtless used by Venutius and his men.

At a crossing track (777734) turn right and along to a gate where you must bear left once over the Scar edge (the $2\frac{1}{2}$ inch map a little inaccurate here), finding a rocky path over the pavements that emerges at a little gorge at Beggar's Stile (777726). The path now descends spectacularly into Crummackdale, an area full of interesting ice-age "erratics," freak gritstone boulders carried by glacier action and left like strange modern sculptures on pedestals of softer rock. The path winds through bracken, broadening into a track to Crummack Farm. Go along the lane from here, but bear left down a fork into a delightful green track which crosses Austwick Beck at an ancient ford and clapper bridge. Join the narrow packhorse track, Moughton Lane, and drop down to the tiny and pretty hamlet of Wharfe. Turn right in Wharfe to the lane and right again towards Austwick, but take the next track right, Thwaite Lane. This is another old and attractive green lane that climbs, with pleasant views, under the great white nob of Norber Scar and enters Clapham village by the two curious tunnels under the Ingleborough estate near Clapham Church.

Maps: One Inch Sheet 90; $2\frac{1}{2}$ inch Sheets SD76, SD77.
Sources: A. Raistrick: "The Pennine Dales" (1968).
*   "Romans in Yorkshire" (1965).*

4: *Romano-British Yorkshire*

Grass Wood—4 miles.

THE victories of the Romans did not completely destroy the Brigantian spirit. Some of the Brigantes did manage to co-exist peacefully with the conquerors, forming the so-called Romano-British culture illustrated in Yorkshire by the setting up of a Roman-British capital as Isurium Brigantum, or modern Aldborough near Boroughbridge. But others were more defiant and kept up active and nagging resistance to the Romans—resistance that exploded every so often to major violence, a kind of guerilla warfare from secret hideouts. Grass Wood was surely such a place. From more peaceful times iron age field boundaries are still visible upon Lea Green or High Pasture.

Start from Grassington Bridge (SD999639), the field path beginning on the Grassington side of the river some 20 yards uphill and soon curving to the riverside. You will soon discover circular yellow waymarks put there by Grassington Group of the Ramblers' Association and providing a most helpful indication and reassurance on your route—a service that Ramblers hope to extend to other popular areas. Through stiles and a tiny footbridge the path reaches Gaistrill's Strid, a superb part of Wharfedale with thin woodland and the river rushing through a broad and shallow gorge. Continue by the riverside under the shadow of Netherside Hall; this path is part of the proposed Dales Way, a splendid 73 mile footpath from Ilkley to Windermere. As the wood thins out, bear right with the path to the stile leading into Grass Wood Lane (983653).

Continue along the lane for about 300 yards. On the right is the entrance to Grass Wood, with a Forestry Commission sign. In addition to its many historical associations, Grass Wood is of course an important nature reserve. Enjoy the profusion of shrub, tree and plant life growing out of the thin limestone soil, but avoid straying from the path and in no circumstances pick or uproot flowers. The track climbs slowly. Ignore an obvious path to the right, but at the top of the track

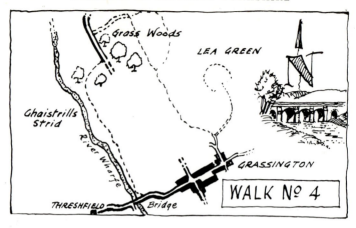

where it becomes a narrow way through wilderness look for a helpful waymark on a tree ahead and turn right. This is a high level path with magnificent views over Wharfedale; it finds its way between ridges of limestone. The high point on the right is Gregory Scar, and soon a green Ministry of Works sign indicates a site of national importance (991653), Gregory Fort below the scar. Little remains to be seen on the ground, but the site has astonishing atmosphere—a deep and rocky valley still thickly wooded, a perfect hiding place and stronghold. The path descends ever deeper through the woodland, emerging at a place (995651) marked as Settlement where presumably a village developed close to the sanctuary of the wood.

Cross a tall ladder stile into mundane daylight, and go straight ahead to a gate and muddy lane. Where the lane bears right take the stile ahead climbing up the hillside and leading to the farm (001645) at the end of Chapel Street, Grassington. To explore Lea Green turn left just before the chapel (003643). Go up Intake Lane, a stony track that leads to an area of open pasture (005654) covered with a criss-cross of low grassy ridges. The careful observer will be able to make out patterns of fields and dwelling areas. A footpath leads from the pasture bottom back into the village.

Maps: One Inch Sheet 90; 2½ Inch sheets SD96, SE06.
Sources: Arthur Raistrick: "Prehistoric Yorkshire" (1965).
"Romans in Yorkshire" (1965).
John Crowther: "Sylva Gars." (1930).

5: *Roman Yorkshire*

Wade's Causeway—6 miles.

THE secret of the Roman domination of Yorkshire lay in the great road system—and nowhere in the North of England is there a more exciting stretch of uncovered Roman military road than on Wheeldale Moor near Goathland. Once known as Wade's Causeway or Wade's Wife Causey after some forgotten Cleveland giant, it can be reached easily from Goathland. This six mile circular walk takes in some dramatic scenery.

Park at the car-park in Goathland, or get off the bus at the Mallyan Spout. Ramblers from Teesside can use the rail services from Middlesbrough, walking along the old Beckhole railway line from Goathland. From the parish church continue to the Pickering-Egton cross-roads, noting the small "pinfold" straight opposite to collect stray sheep and cattle in the village. There is a choice of ways here. According to the map, a bridle road goes to Hunt House by the Roman road. This path starts clearly enough, up a low green ridge almost exactly in the centre of the triangle of land between the two roads. At a fork bear right along the narrower path to a low green shooting butt. But beyond here it is quite untraceable on the ground, though the determined fellwalker used to bracken and heather should be able to make his way fairly well along the line of the track till it becomes more discernible near the ravine above Hunt House (825987). Much less strenuously, one can simply keep to the grassy verge of the Egton Road, turning left at the cross roads and along the lane to Hunt House.

From Hunt House the lane becomes a stony track to the Wheeldale Youth Hostel, and plentiful signs indicate the "Goathland" Roman Road. The path continues through a gate and then crosses Wheeldale Beck at a highly attractive ravine. The broad track straight ahead is the Lyke WakeWalk; avoid this, keeping to the path on the left climbing diagonally to where notices indicate the Roman Road on the moortop. It is worth every inch of the climb, for here is a broad and slightly cambered highway, beautifully preserved in the sandy

21

subsoil, curving over the far moorland in a most authoritative manner. It once led directly to the important practice camps at Cawthorne, near Pickering, and possibly on to Malton to enable legions quickly to reinforce the coastal garrisons at the time of attack, which in later years of the Empire was frequent. The road itself was probably built in the first century, and apart from the loss of top stones has changed little in appearance.

Descend again down to the stepping stones over Wheeldale Beck, but do not return back to Hunt House. Instead climb straight ahead along the broad and clear path of the Lyke Wake Walk, that modern pilgrim's way, up to Simon Howe clearly marked by a tall cairn on the horizon straight ahead. This is a steady climb rewarded by fine views of the Tabular Hills. At Simon Howe (830982) you have reached a Bronze Age Tumulus or Round Barrow. According to Frank Elgee, the middle Bronze Age or Urn people would have co-existed with the Romans. Fascinating to realise, as you turn left and due northwards at the cairn, that this ancient Bronze Age track has been in constant use at least these last three thousand years, and continued to be an important road from Whitby for smugglers and packhorse men right up to the building of the turnpikes. But look across to the mysterious twin hillocks of Two Howes (825994), Bronze Age barrows which now act as fine waymarks. This is not a coincidence. It ws the custom of the Urn people to bury their princes on some high and lonely eminence where all should see them, and close to their high-ways to guide them through the mortal dangers of storm and darkness. You may well be grateful for those noble spirits'

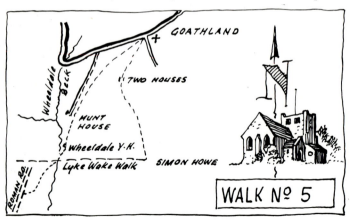

What the walker seeks to avoid. Bank Holiday Monday scene at Goathland, starting point of this walk to Wade's Causeway. (Geoffrey N. Wright)

guidance on a wild day. When I last reached Two Howes a marvellous double rainbow blazed across the surrounding moorland. When you finally descend along the easily discernible track and past a narrow greenish tarn towards Goathland, the scattered little village and even the Roman Road seem quite prosaic in comparison.

Maps: One Inch - North York Moors Tourist; Sheet 92 or 86.
2½ Inch Sheets NZ80, SE89.
Sources: Frank Elgee: "Early Man in North East Yorkshire"
(1930).
H.M.S.O. "Regional Guide to Ancient Monuments:
Northern England" (1951).

6:   *Saxon Yorkshire*

Kirkdale—8 miles.

MOST of modern Yorkshire contains the basic settlement
pattern of those sturdy Teutonic settlers, Angles and
Vikings, who cleared most of what must have been primeval
wilderness to build their homesteads. The actual foundations
of their farms, hamlets and villages are still a living part of
our contemporary countryside. Likewise, footpaths, lanes and
tracks across what once were open fields pre-date enclosures
by a full millenium. The modern Celtic, Anglian or Viking
names, often little corrupted, reflect early settlements and
fords. The prefix Kirk or Kirby for instance implies an Anglian
Christian settlement with a church being overtaken by Viking
invaders, who may in some places have actually destroyed the
primitive wooden churches.

Kirkby Moorside is just such a little town, easily reached
via the A170 Helmsley-Pickering road or by the none-too-
frequent United Ripon-Scarborough bus. From the market
square continue uphill and left above the square along the
Farndale road. Look out for a narrow metalled lane forking
off at a slight angle to the left (SE 693866) and entering a new
housing estate. Bear left beside a crescent of grass to a path
between houses; where this swings left back to Kirkby Moorside climb a fence-stile (i.e. a low fence designed to be climbed)
on the right, crossing the pasture ahead parallel to a row of
tall trees and reaching a second fence-stile. Cross fields now
(some may be ploughed) keeping a fairly straight line ahead
over fence stiles; villagers use this path so it isn't too difficult
to see on the ground. As you approach the edge of Snapes
Wood, make for the bottom left hand corner of the field
below the wood to a large ash tree (675862). Cross the fence-
stile this side of the tree, continuing along the hedge to the
next field corner where another fence-stile leads to a little green
ravine. Go along the bottom here, the white signpost in the
lane indicating the line of path which emerges at a gate.

Follow the sign along the lane to St. Gregory's Minster.
Note the caves in the rock on the right just before you descend

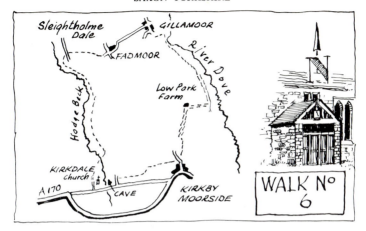

to the little ford—this is the famous Kirkdale Cave where many prehistoric remains were once discovered. Cross the ford by the footbridge, turning first right at the top towards the little Minster (677858). This superb building dates from the late Saxon period, and has one detail of national importance— the longest extant inscription in stone in Old English in the country. It is on a sundial, now kept over the doorway in the porch, telling how "Orm the son of Gamal bought St. Gregorius' Minster when it was all broken and fallen and he has let it make new from the ground in Edward's days the King, and Tosti's days the Earl" (i.e. about 1060) "Hawarth me wrohte & Brand prs" (i.e. Haworth and Brand, priests, made me—the sundial).

Kirkdale is still a lovely valley, thickly wooded in places, though ubiquitous spruce replace the older trees as the foresters' saws buzz through the valley. The frequent patches of newly felled woodland, ugly as they are, must have been familiar to Anglian eyes. The path continues behind the Minster on the green sward, bearing right to a little bridge over the Hodge Beck and continuing between river and forestry plantation up the valley to Hold Caldron. Take the gate on the left, ignoring the slightly misleading private sign. The path is along the forestry road between river and wood, winding round the gorge with fine views up-stream. But where the forestry track climbs right and uphill into the forestry plantation (661878), leave the track and keep along the open pasture bottom. A quarter mile or so later a gateway ahead leads to a narrow path climbing through woodland, with

25

pretty views over a steep gorge and round into Sleightholme-dale. This name implies a Viking settlement, probably where the fine farmstead of Sleightholmedale is seen ahead. At the narrow lane turn right uphill. After a couple of hundred yards, before a roadside quarry, look for a path (667887) just past a scraggy holly tree. It climbs up a gap in the rocky hillside to a small gate; follow the hedge at the top, going over the fence-stile at the bottom of the field and through gaps or fence-stiles to Fadmoor. A new pipeline has complicated the line of path a little, but the village is an excellent bearing.

At Fadmoor, cross the village green and go along the lane for half a mile to Gillamoor. Turn right at the *Royal Oak* towards Kirkby, but take the first track left past the village cricket ground. Go left through a gate here, just under some small pylons (685892) to a green bridle way that soon swings right and drops down to a wood. About sixty yards below the gate look for a tiny path on the right; it is well used but narrow and climbs back up the woodland. This path is a delight, following the very edge of pasture and woodland with intriguing views through the treetops over the lower part of Farndale and the hills beyond. It is distinguished by a series of little gates, with only one low fence to cross. The ragged scrubland through which it winds recalls the kind of wilder-ness of Anglian times, full of wild life with only small clearings of arable land to intrude. One only hopes that in the name of efficiency modern foresters won't be quick to clear the area for the inevitable neat rows of conifer. But one scarcely com-plains when the path enters a deep arch of spruce and pine woodland finally to join a broader forestry ride.

At the next junction (703878) turn right along a tarmac track to Low Park Farm. Don't enter the farm, but turn left along the lane by cottages and through gates until Kirkby Moorside is again in sight on the edge of the plain. Where the track swings right and the way is unenclosed on your left (697870), leave it to make straight ahead dropping to the bot-tom left hand corner of the pasture. Cross a little syke and make for the churchyard ahead. A small gate on the left leads into the churchyard; turn right by the church and out of the iron gate to find Kirkby's ancient market cross in a little court just behind the Market Square.

Maps: One Inch Sheet 92; 2½ Inch Sheet SE68, 78.
Sources: Nikolaus Pevsner: "The North Riding" (1966).
Arthur Raistrick (ed.): "The North York Moors National Park" (1966).

7: *Norman Yorkshire*

R ICHMOND is the most beautiful country town in the North of England—architecturally rich with superb medieval eighteenth and nineteenth century buildings and houses, and even a couple of twentieth century buildings that earn mention in Penvser. It is a living town, in no way "arty" or sickly picturesque but tough and vigorous. Its close links with Catterick Camp still keep the military associations evoked by its massive Norman castle, founded by Alan the Red, friend of the Conqueror, and containing probably the oldest great hall in Britain dating from the eleventh century. The tall keep of the castle still dominates the entrance of Swaledale. Visit the elegant fourteenth or fifteenth century Franciscan tower of Greyfriars or the splendid little Georgian theatre (preferably an actual performance).

This short excursion into Richmondshire, as it was known in former times, begins at the castle. Go left, following the Castle Walk sign, and down the steep but short street with its cottages huddled round the castle wall. It turns right onto a high promenade below the sheer drop of the walls, with dramatic views across the river and falls to open countryside. Even to the present day the town shelters in the lea of the old Norman keep. At the finger posts at the end of Castle Walk, find the cobbled snicket winding round to the left by the inn. To the left again under a masonry arch down the steep Cornforth Hill to Bar Gate Green below. Descend and cross the fine bridge.

The path into Swaledale is to the right below the cottage (NZ 170005) and along the riverside. It soon climbs slightly and gives unforgettable views along the Dale which, if Wharfedale and Dentdale aren't too fresh in the memory, is arguably England's finest. The path, very well used and easy to discern, follows the massive gorge round a rough S-shape and enters a National Trust woodland. Sometimes it goes through pleasant woodland, and at other times through pasture. After about a mile and a half of extremely attractive walking it emerges below

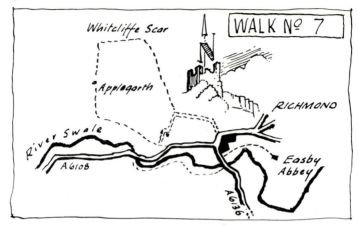

a flight of steps at a white waterworks buildings and a bridge over the river (146007). Turn right back towards Richmond.

There is no legal right of way along the other side of the river here; one should perhaps face the traffic on the narrow and highly dangerous A6108. However, if you enter the first gate on your right, keeping to the edge of the field and working right round to the riverside past a small river board hut, an "unofficial" footpath is soon discernible. It goes over a little footbridge and becomes an extremely attractive riverside walk. The path winds past some broad and rocky shallows by the edge of the river and climbs up with a view of a caravan site ahead; look for a fork left that climbs to a little gate by a lay-bye (155008). Cross the road and enter the farm track straight opposite, climbing back left uphill. For energetic souls wanting a longer walk into Swaledale this leads to a fine river-side path, eventually climbing up past Applegarth Farm (129016) and onto the dramatic heights of Whitcliffe Scar and a high-level walk back to Richmond. But if you've spent a good part of the morning exploring Richmond, then you will be happy enough to climb up the first green lane to the right. This takes you uphill, zig-zagging past a little farm. At the lane top (154015) turn right and back to Richmond, passing woodland and a lovely open parkland entered by little stiles in the fence. Keep your height here to enjoy superb views across the old Norman garrison—that tall, grey and square tower still defending the Dale. And at the end of the park re-enter the lane, descending to the centre of Richmond.

Maps: One Inch Sheet 91; *2½ Inch Sheet NZ*10.

8: *Monastic Times*

IS there anywhere more exciting and evocative than Fountains Abbey? One of the richest and most powerful Cistercian houses in the country and precursor of the enormous commercial enterprise that formed Yorkshire's greatness, something of its wealth and influence is reflected in the great medieval port of York which was the natural outlet for Fountain's wealth, mostly wool. It remains as one of the most beautiful monastic ruins in Europe set in eighteenth century landscape gardens of taste and style.

Start from Ripon, itself a market town of enormous historic interest with its Minster with Saxon crypt and the medieval Wakeman's house. Go down Skellgate, the street at the corner of the town square by the Wakeman's house. Just over the river bridge go through a gap stile and a tiny park. Bear right along a lane that soon becomes a track and eventually a footpath by the Skell through woodland. Where the woodland thins out, look for the path's continuation ahead and slightly to the left by the ruins of a footpath sign (SE 301702). It now re-enters woodland along a sunken way that seems to have been part of a forgotten canal project. This emerges at a track; turn right over a stile and down to a footbridge with a little gate over the river (299699). Follow the obvious path ahead for a few yards up the slope but almost immediately turn left through a field gate on the brow of the little hill. The path is alongside a hedge on the left and through gates, emerging on a track almost directly opposite Plumpton Hall (291697).

Go left along this track descending through woodland to the river again; don't cross the ford but keep to the right fork and enter Mackershaw woods by means of a stile. The path goes through the wood and emerges in the Studley Royal estate and the superb "Valley of the Seven Bridges"—a series of low ornamental bridges where the river, often dry and stony in places, is forded. It passes fine tall chestnuts and crosses the river at the end of Studley Park lake by a long footbridge. The estate, now owned by the County Council, was landscaped

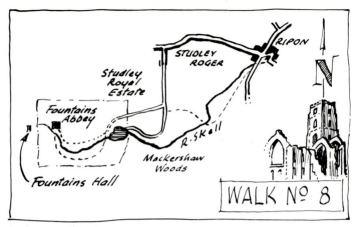

by John Aislebie.

Enter the Abbey grounds, a charge being payable here. The grounds are open throughout the year, but close before dusk which is quite early in winter time. Take the path left off the main track, which winds round the fine ornamental lakes and canal, to enjoy the celebrated "surprise" view of the Abbey with a grey reflection in the still waters of the canal. The ruins cannot fail to impress with their scale and beauty—the great tower with its many gargoyles, the enormous cloisters with their delicate supports, the chapterhouses and the kitchens are particularly memorable features. Do not omit to visit Fountains Hall just outside the West Gate (your ticket gives re-admission to the grounds), a delightful example of Jacobean domestic architecture showing early neo-Classical influence.

Return through the grounds, especially delightful in January and February with banks of wild snowdrops. Once outside the East Gate walk along the drive keeping right towards Studley Roger or wander freely over the open parkland as you choose. The county council keep herds of roe and fallow deer on the estate. At the ornamented gates turn left into the village. The path back to Ripon starts at the village centre opposite the bus stop by the letter box in a house wall (290703). This is a pleasant path through pasture marked by kissing gates, passing a football ground and eventually emerging on the road about half a mile above Ripon.

Maps: One Inch Sheet 91; 2½ Inch Sheets SE27, SE37.
Sources: Charles H. Moody: "Fountains Abbey." (1965).
*   Nikolaus Pevsner: "The West Riding" (1963).*

9:   *Late Monastic*

Mount Grace Priory—7 miles.

OSMOTHERLEY is a pleasant little village just below the great tableland of the Cleveland Hills. This circular walk on the edge of the plateau uses two of the long-distance footpaths of the area, and descends to visit the unique Carthusian monastery of Mount Grace.

Park in a quiet spot in Osmotherley village. There is an infrequent United bus from Northallerton, and Leeds-Middlesbrough buses stop at Clack lane ends, the cross roads on the A19 Middlesbrough-Thirsk road below the village. Turn left at the market cross and, climbing past the last cottages in the village, ignore the track to Lady Chapel but take the next metalled way left by a "no unauthorised vehicles" sign (SE 457977). This climbs steadily uphill, through gates and past a couple of farms; there are fine views of the bleak wastes of Osmotherley Moor to the right and behind you the great mound of Black Hambleton—the medieval waste of Blackamoor. Follow the track left towards the television station, but go right between fence and stone wall past the Trig station which is the start of the 45 mile Lyke Wake Walk. There are spectacular views across the great Vale of Mowbray here, with the industry of Teesside forming a smudge on the horizon. The path turns eastwards and descends to a gate with a Moors Path sign to indicate that you are now also on the Cleveland way. This is Britain's second long-distance footpath, a hundred miles of magnificent North York Moors and coastal walking. Follow the Way downhill across open moorland along the very well-beaten track to Scarth Nick (NZ 474004).

Leave both the Lyke Wake and the Cleveland Way here, turning left in the lane. Look just to the left of the cattle grid for an unofficial bridle path dropping down the hillside to rejoin the lane again at the junction. Take the narrow lane to the left towards Potto; this is a delightfully winding wooded way for a good half mile. As the road bends right follow a bridle path to the left, signposted to Osmotherley (472013).

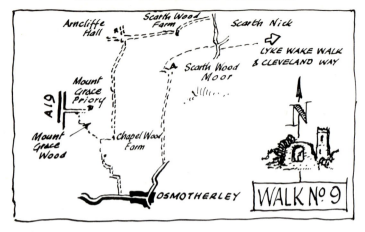

This lovely route winds by farmland and forestry plantation past Scarth Nick and Scarth Lees farm. At Scarth Wood farm look for its continuation as a green way at the far side of the farmhouse. There are continuing pleasant views across the plain from under the hanging scar of Arncliffe Wood over towards the village of Ingleby Arncliffe with its newer skirt of Teesside suburbia. When your path climbs and enters a broader forestry track (455006), go left for a few yards to reach the steep green ascent past cypress trees and back on to a broad new track. This is a steady high-level walk now, looking southwards and westwards with the grey outline of the distant Pennines almost certainly visible ahead.

Once out of the trees, Chapel Wood farm is just ahead. You have now rejoined the Cleveland Way which has taken a more direct route from the top of Arncliffe Wood. At Chapel Wood Farm (SE 453980) bear right and take the gate to the left leading to the vestiges of a green lane by the fieldside below the farm. Take care here. You pass a narrow tongue of wood just above a tiny streamlet on your left as you descend the field. In the left hand corner of the field, find the rather rickety remains of a stile (448980) which leads to an overgrown but most impressive path, tricky yet delightful and running through dense woodland. Follow it to the right for a hundred yards or so keeping parallel with the hillside; the going is a shade slippy in places. The path then plunges through delightful arches of slender trees and downhill to a tiny broken footbridge and stile over a seep at the bottom of Mount Grace Wood. Go straight ahead over the field here, turning right at the field top to Mount Grace Farm and the drive to the Priory.

Founded in 1398, this is a Charterhouse or monastery of the Carthusians, a late and strict order of monks who practised vows of silence and denied even visual contact with their brethren. Each monk dwelt in a separate cell, with his own water supply, lavatory and tiny garden. Specially designed hatches allowed food to be deposited without even a hand being seen. It is an extraordinarily moving experience in our pleasure-loving and secular age to stand in the ruins of one of the little cells, with the sky and the wooded hills visible above, and to imagine that remote and stoical existence. The ruins are open most days. Bus travellers can return to Osmotherley by a service from the lane end, but most walkers must find their way back through Mount Grace Wood. Care and strong lungs are needed for the steep climb. At the top of the wood continue in the same direction for a hundred yards or so to find a wood and wire gap stile in the fence on the right (450980) which observant souls will have noticed on their way down. The path is below a small farm, soon joining the farm track as it curves left towards Osmotherley. As the track swings right into the village, a tiny path straight ahead emerges at a cottage with a curious ark-like roof.

Maps: One Inch Sheet 91; $2\frac{1}{2}$ *Inch Sheets NZ* 40, *SE* 49
Sources: Nikolaus Pevsner: The North Riding (1966).

Mount Grace Priory, considered to be the finest Carthusian monastic remains in the country. (Geoffrey N. Wright).

33

Castle Bolton—6 miles.

NO visitor to Wensleydale can fail to be impressed by Castle Bolton, that enormous fortified house and castle built by Richard, Lord Scrope, Chancellor of Richard II at the end of the fourteenth century. This walk satisfyingly combines a visit to the castle with a visit to Aysgarth Falls, the impressive series of shallow falls that have long been a major attraction in the northern Dales. The village is served by United buses, and motorists should park at the NRCC official car park and new information centre at the Bear Park by the old railway (SE 010886).

Having perhaps explored the nature trail and the Higher Falls, take the well signposted footpath leaving the bend of the road just above the bridge to the middle and then on to the Lower Falls. Both look very impressive through the trees. Past Lower Falls the path clearly waymarked by large white arrows, bears left uphill across a stile and past Hollin House Farm. Follow the track beyond the farm, bearing right alongside the fence. Quite soon you reach a stile in the wall in the right by a makeshift sign. The status of the next path is a little vague, but it is possibly an old "county" road. Turn right at the stile, going straight across the pasture to another stile, and entering an enclosed green lane through a gate (029899). Pass below Sunny Bank by a small building and on to Low Thoresby Farm, looking for a little gap stile to the left (036905). This gives access to a fieldpath, again marked by stiles in the walls to the cross roads in the lane just below Castle Bolton. Go straight up the lane to the castle, or perhaps take a tiny bridle path, green and a little overgrown, starting a few hundred yards past the junction (024911) and climbing uphill past the old railway to the village.

Castle Bolton is the most romantic of castles—partially ruined, full of ravens, wallflowers, skeleton towers, gloomy dungeons, rusting cannons and offering superb views of Pen Hill. At the same time it is partially preserved and retains passages, stairways, and enormous medieval banqueting halls.

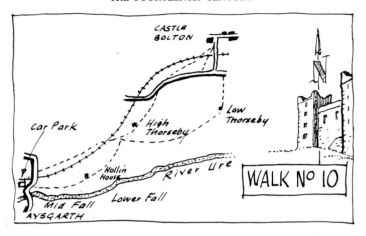

This great fortified house has played a notable part in English history, being the only surviving castle outside London where Mary Queen of Scots was imprisoned (in 1568/9). The castle is open to the public, and has a small folk museum and an excellent restaurant as an additional attraction.

To return to Aysgarth you might be tempted to walk along the old Northallerton-Hawes railway line, reached by a little white gate just below Castle Bolton. The line was, unfortunately, sold in small sections into private ownership some years ago and no public right of way exists along what until very recently was a public asset. But there is little physical bar to access, the land being of no agricultural value, and in four places where underpasses segment the line continuity can be maintained by simply scrambling up and down the embankment. At the time of writing the North Riding County Council is considering purchasing the line, initially as far as Aysgarth from Castle Bolton. It has enormous recreational potential as a linear park, footpath, cycling and bridleway and nature trail on the lines of Derbyshire County Council's Tissington Trail in the Peak District. The line is historically interesting and scenically superb, giving magnificent views—far better than from existing footpaths—across to Penhill and down Bishopdale and Walden. It contains the kind of mixture of embankment and cutting that, according to the recent Countryside Commission *Appleton* report, forms the type of route needed in an area of high recreational demand and high amenity value.

The official path is less interesting and bears right at the crossing of the old bridleway over the railway (035914). It makes its way roughly diagonally across the pasture, through gap stiles in the walls, to farm buildings in the lane corner—it is necessary to scramble over the milk churn stand into the lane. Walk along the lane for a quarter of a mile or so and then turn left (028907) along an unfenced farm track, soon turning through a gap stile on your right to reach the farmyard of High Thoresby. Continue in the same direction through the gate at the back of the farm towards a gap stile in the wall ahead, and then a second gap stile to the right which was passed earlier. Don't return via Hollin unless you want a second view of the falls. Bear right across a "level crossing" over the old railway, turning left parallel with the railway embankment and under a surviving bridge. Go along the other side of the railway, descending through dampish woodland to emerge on the lane just above the falls.

Maps: One Inch Sheet 90;   2½ *Inch Sheets SE*08, *SE*09.
Sources: George Jackson: The Story of Bolton Castle (1956).
      J. H. Appleton: Disused Railways in the countryside of England and Wales (1970).

Castle Bolton, as seen looking up Wensleydale with a stormy sky overhead.
(John Edenbrow)

The Wars of the Roses

Towton Field—11 miles.

ON Palm Sunday, 1461, in the gentle rolling country south west of York, there occurred the most terrible single battle of the Wars of the Roses—the Battle of Towton. The Lancastrians were defeated at an appalling cost to both sides, thus ensuring the reign of the Yorkist Kings. Contemporary estimates put the number of dead on that freezing day at well over 20,000—it was said that the waters of the little river Cock turned red with blood, and this seems no exaggeration. Many of the most famous warrior lords in the land including Lords Clifford and Dacre and the Earls of Devonshire and Wiltshire perished in the carnage. Even to this day meadows to the north of the battlefield are known as "bloody meadow" and older maps show the stump of the Bur Tree from which Lord Dacre was shot, not far from his monument on the Towton-Saxton road.

Begin at Tadcaster, an attractive old coaching town in spite of the brewery smell and the traffic on the A64. Walk along the Leeds road, past the A162 junction, noting the old turnpike milestone on your left before turning left along the Stutton road. As it is no longer possible to use an "unofficial" path along the lines of the old railway to Stutton, you must continue along Stutton Road through suburbia taking the signposted tarmac path that leads by the railway to the village. Keep ahead along the main street, turn right by the chapel and over the old railway crossing (SE 479414) and then fork left past bungalows onto a brick path that is soon a rough track up Wingate Hill. This joins a track above a farm; go left here, forking right along Chantry Lane and noting a wayside cross about right. This lane is a medieval "pilgrims way" leading to the thirteenth century chapel at Hazelwood; it soon becomes a pleasant stony way through fields which, if one ignores the pylons, are reverting to something like their medieval appearance as hedgerows vanish under the plough.

Follow the lane to Hazelwood Castle, a distance of over a mile, noting the track to Hazelwood Lodge Farm (454400) not

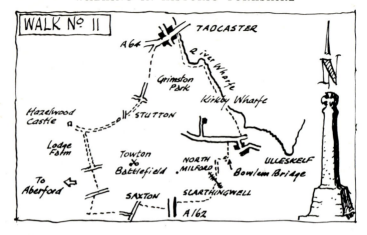

far from the castle, which unfortunately is normally closed to the public. However one can see a good deal of the buildings from the outside; they are an incredible mixture of the medieval and the eighteenth century. Retrace your steps to the Hazelwood Lodge Farm track, turning southwards through arable fields. The track winds slightly left past the farm buildings, through a gate, and climbs over a low ridge before descending through Newstead Farm. It goes over a beck, climbing up to join another track coming in from the right. Turn left here, but pause to look across the valley to your left to Castle Hill Wood —a key point in the Battle of Towton which raged across the tiny valley between this point and Tadcaster. Take the first gate on the right (463378) to a rather overgrown green way by a hedge. This climbs another low ridge to join the path from Aberford, continuing to Lead Hall and tiny Lead Church almost opposite—an austere fourteenth century chapel carefully restored and worth a visit.

Across the road from Lead Church is the *Crooked Billet Inn* (454367). A public path follows the hedgerow along the low hill just behind and to the left of the whitestone building behind the inn, crossing the hedge at the top and then following a succession of illegally ploughed paths. Make for gaps in the hedges about 10 yards to the south of a line of wooden pylons. These lead on to a stile entering a long pasture—a small white building is your bearing in the centre of Saxton village. An easier route, with less ploughing, is to follow the green lane to the right of the inn, keeping to the left of the hedge where this peters out. Turn left along the hedge at the top of the field towards a copse by pylons on the line of the medieval way which is soon joined by the modern road into Saxton. This is a delightful village. Spend some time at the late Norman church just behind the old *Greyhound Inn* where you will discover Lord Dacre's tomb, a rare example of an outdoor fifteenth century sarcophagus, in front of the church.

Continue by the Manor House Farm with its fine doorway creast, reached by a track between cottages a few yards south of the church. Follow the track by the hedge; where it peters out keep the same direction across ploughed land to emerge, if you are on course, through a little copse. Just at the south side of this, stone steps lead to the road in an area known, for some reason, as Dinting Dale (487370). Turn left, taking the lane ahead and to the right to Scarthingwell. Past this hamlet this becomes a track and then a bridle path known as Moor Lane. Keep left at a junction by a dense narrow wood, finally emerging on to the old railway line. The path continues straight ahead to North Milford.

Follow the lane from North Milford up to the late seventeenth century Hall (506395). Take the second gate on the right, entering into narrow pasture which turns out to be the last vestiges of an ancient lane with just visible cobbles. It leads by a gate to Bowlam Bridge (509395), where concrete covers any sign of the medieval. Follow the green path along the dyke top to join a track through arable land, passing a hedge and then bearing left to the Ulleskelf road. Turn right towards the railway but fork left before the bridge (infrequent rail services between Leeds and York, from the station), following the track to a bridge over the beck (518403). Look for a stile on the left, and follow a fieldpath bearing left and crossing fence-stiles or going through gaps. The route across the second field is a little muddy and over the third is close to a reed bed; it finally joins the flood dyke path at a stile just behind the hamlet of Kirkby Wharfe (509411). There is lovely riverside walking now beside the Wharfe.

Take a little care at two points (502420 and 500422) where the path avoids circuitous bends in the river. Cross the bridge over Cock Beck, noting the ruins of Kettleman Bridge where once the now diverted Cock Beck ran. Enter the busy town of Tadcaster—in medieval times an important little port at the highest navigable point of the Wharfe—by means of a couple of gates and an avenue of trees opposite the town's fine eighteenth century bridge.

Maps: One Inch Sheet 97; $2\frac{1}{2}$ *Inch Sheet SE*43, 44.

Norton Tower—8 miles.

THE old market town of Skipton is a microcosm of York-shire's history with its Norman stronghold guarding the Aire Gap, country market, early industrial revolution canal, cotton mill and railway facilities. The different ages of Skipton co-exist in a background of splendid countryside. But it is the memory of the great family of Clifford, Tudor lords, which still dominates the town, and is most vividly focused in the fine castle repaired by Anne Clifford, Countess of Pembroke, in the seventeenth century as a tribute to her celebrated fore-fathers.

This walk might begin after a visit to the castle which is open daily. Turn left past the church at the top of the main street onto the Settle road and towards the canal bridge. Go right down the steps onto the towpath of the old Springs Branch of the Leeds-Liverpool canal. This follows the line of the ancient moat under the enormous impregnable rock face on which the castle is built. The path is soon a fascinating raised way between stream and canal with a waterfall to the left. Cross the bridge at the end of the canal and enter a lane by house gardens; go left here down the track with sudden views back along the canal and over the old town. Just past a fine old warehouse turn right (SD 989521) up Chapel Hill towards the lane end and white footpath sign. Go over the stile and make your way up the hillside, keeping straight ahead to a second stone stile. Enjoy splendid views all round from this point in the Old Park, once part of the castle grounds. Particularly impressive is the view back over the town, still extremely compact between a huge bowl of surrounding hills. Look for an old ladder stile on the line of path, slightly to the right but almost directly below you. This emerges on a narrow metalled lane, and continues for just a few yards on the right soon crossing a golf course as signs will indicate. Keep straight ahead, over a complex of stiles slightly to the left, and along a hedge to a stile in a narrow lane. Turn left here to the Grassing-ton road and then, passing the footpath sign straight ahead, continue slightly right through pasture roughly parallel with the overhead cables to meet the lane from Stirton just behind a cattle pond.

Follow the lane round three bends, and at the last of these look for a gate on the left leading to a track over the moor (975539). As the track bears left, keep straight ahead. The odd marker post and eventually the summit of Sharp Haw give useful bearings. Soon you are scrambling over a rickety stile onto the summit with its white trig station (959553). Sharp Haw may be a mere 1,171 feet, but it gives superb panoramic views of the surrounding fells, looking on the right up into the National Park and Barden Moor and Fell. The Aire Gap with the shimmering serpentine canal coursing through the drumlins can be seen to the left.

Bear right through an opening in the stone wall. The next quarter of a mile is a shade tricky. Make your way off the summit, crossing a steep little ravine. Where an obvious track

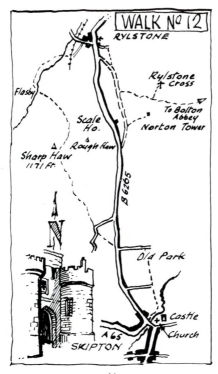

41

The gaunt remains of Norton Tower form a striking skyline above Rylstone.
(W. R. Mitchell)

continues through a gate, strike sharp right across the bracken in the direction of Rough Haw and go through a gateway. Keep to the wall on the right, edging round a small ravine to a second gateway. Bear left at about 45 degrees from here to a gate which leads to a green lane, soon becoming a deep sunken way as it enters Flasby with the path keeping to the lane shoulder. Just past the stream enter the first gate on the right (947566), fording a beck below a barn and going along by Eshton beck across a farm track. Where a tributary stream-let bars your way, follow it left for a dozen yards or so to where it can be crossed easily (953575). Directly behind is a low fence; cross this and keep straight ahead, the stream entering a wooded gorge on the right. At the top of the slope is a gate. Continue through stiles and as the gorge opens out lose height gently, looking for the second footbridge over the stream at the beginning of a second stretch of woodland (960580). Up the slope is a sunken track which soon bears right over a bridge crossing the still used Grassington branch railway. At a junction (966584) turn left through a farm to a small ginnel passing a beech hedge to reach the centre of Rylstone.

This highly attractive village was once the home of another powerful but ill-fated Tudor family, the Nortons, ancient rivals of the Cliffords who lost their entire fortunes in the abortive catholic Rising of the North in 1569—when the Cliffords remained loyal to Elizabeth. The tragedy produced one of the most interesting of Yorkshire's folk tales, the White Doe of Rylstone, skilfully retold by Wordsworth some centuries later. Turn right by the village pond to the Grassington road, going almost directly across towards Rylstone church—a sturdy and typical Dales church with a flagged parishioners' way. Find another parishioners' way past the church, take the second gate on the right (973588), and go straight ahead through stiles and a little wood. Keep directly ahead by a gate and stile into a broad green lane, the old pre-turnpike highway to Skipton and a road doubtless well-known and used by both Cliffords and Nortons. High on the fell to your left is Rylstone Cross, and ahead on a lower hillock jutting out from the hillside is the ruin of Norton Tower.

Here there is a choice of ways. The first gate on the left gives access to an ancient bridle road—undoubtedly used by the monks of Bolton Priory and probably by Emily Norton—which crosses that vast area of heathermoor known as Barden Moor and Fell. This is now open to the public by means of an access agreement with the Duke of Devonshire—an heir to the Clifford fortunes. The enterprising fell walker might plan to walk up to Rylstone Cross or Crookridge Crag, or even back to Skipton by Embsay. Note that no dogs are allowed on the access areas, except of course on the bridle road which is still a public right of way. To visit Norton Tower go through the second gate to a well-used path (not unfortunately a right of way, but the well-behaved visitor is not likely to be troubled) which climbs up to this sturdy ruin which was once a kind of summerhouse for the Nortons (976570). From the end of the green lane at Sandy Beck there are buses back to Skipton. Check the time to avoid a long wait.

Maps: One Inch Sheet 95; 2½ *Inch Sheet SD*95.
Sources: W. H. Dawson: The History of Skipton (1882).
  Geoffrey Rowley: Old Skipton (1969).
  William Wordsworth: The White Doe of Rylstone
                                                    (1815).
  West Riding Ramblers' Association: Roaming round Rylstone (1970).

13:   *The Seventeenth Century*

Stainforth—10 miles.

A S trade grew in the sixteenth and seventeenth centuries, so did patterns of communication. In the days before the turnpikes, strings of packhorses crossed the Pennines and their tracks have remained over the remoter hillsides. They cross rivers and streams by those characteristic and delightful packhorse bridges. This 11 mile walk based on Settle explores some of these ways and bridges.

From the market place in Settle make your way along the Skipton road to the post office, turning right here past the railway station, left at the road end and right at the fork towards the river. Ramblers using Giggleswick station will approach from the opposite direction. Just beyond the river pass a row of houses, and almost at the end of these (SD 813633) look for an opening to the right between gardens. This gives through a wicket gate to a pretty riverside path and on to Settle Bridge. Cross the A65 to the track directly opposite, which leads to a barn. The path continues beyond and is marked by stiles as it passes an attractive gorge of the Ribble above Langcliffe Mill. Where it enters the lane look for the stile almost opposite leading to a curious little path parallel to the lane. It goes past a signpost and woodland behind Stackhouse (814656); as the wood thins out turn sharp left up the hillside to find a stile in the wall above you indicating the line of path. It now bears slightly left through a gap in the next wall, but climbs to the left of the wall corner ahead to a gate. Almost immediately to your left is the round mound of a barrow (806662), probably of Bronze Age date. Follow the wall on your right, going through a gate near the wall corner and then a second gate ahead. Straight ahead is a sheepfold, and from there a good track descends into the hamlet of Feizor.

This tiny settlement grew round a grange of Fountains Abbey. It is more than mere speculation to assume it may have been an important packhorse station in monastic times, once on a main Lancashire-Yorkshire route between Lan-

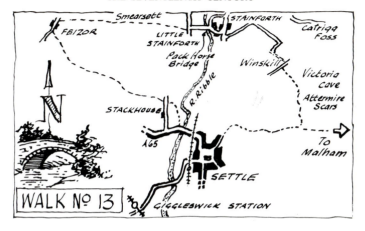

caster (a medieval port) and York, Richmond or Fountains Abbey. Turn right and ford the beck running through the village, taking the next field gate on your right. This leads to pasture, with an old sunken lane visible on your right. Towards the top of the field cross a steep stile on the right; the old packhorse way is soon clearly visible, worn quite distinctly into the hillside by generations of hooves. The path follows the remains of a wall opposite Pot Scar, crosses a stile and then descends. Look for a step stile on the left in the wall ahead, that runs parallel with the direction you are taking. Make for the little ridge top in front, offering unforgettable views of Penyghent and Ribblesdale. Descend rightwards to locate a stile in the wall below you. Take Stainforth village below as a bearing, go over a fence and wire stile, and past a farm to cross the lane to Stainforth Hall and a large caravan site. One reaches the famous packhorse bridge, a structure much more substantial than most. At the road above the bridge turn right to the village, turning right again by the small church and enormous rectory. Toilets are by the car park further along the main road.

Stainforth was, as the name implies, once an important packhorse ford and a junction of routes. Take the tiny path from the bridge at the right of Stainforth Beck. Go past the post office and up Goat Scar Lane. At the summit cross the stile to the left which leads down to Catrigg Force, a narrow gorge with a tall waterfall of immense beauty. Back on Goat Scar Lane continue through the gate ahead, bearing left along a grassy track to Winskill (829666) and turning right at the tarmac drive via Langcliffe Scar to the Malham road. Go right for a few yards, but once over the cattle grid bear left along a faint track over moorland. Look for a gap in the wall on the left after a couple of hundred yards. This leads to the path past Victoria Cave—where remains of Palaeolithic man and prehistoric animals were discovered—to the spectacular gorge of Attermire Scar.

This path now enters the Settle-Malham packhorse track, a route that had its continuation in the celebrated Mastiles lane towards Wharfedale. Keep to the Attermire side of the wall at the rough building which was once an old rifle range, soon bearing right up the pasture to join a clear and obvious track through gates. This eventually descends dramatically into Ribblesdale and over the rooftops of Settle.

Maps: One Inch Sheet 90; 2½ Inch Sheets SD86, SD76.
Sources: Arthur Raistrick: Green Tracks on the Pennines (1962).

The sylvan surroundings of Stainforth bridge, one of the most picturesque crossings of the Ribble. (G. H. Hesketh)

46

14:   *The Eighteenth Century*

Coxwold—12 miles.

LAURENCE STERNE, author of that comic masterpiece *Tristram Shandy*, wrote of his native vale of Coxwold: "O' tis a delicious retreat both from its beauty and air of solitude." It hasn't changed a lot since Sterne's day—the villages are as lovely as ever.

Start at Kilburn, reached off the A170 at Thirsk before Sutton Bank or by using the United Ripon-Helmsley bus. Kilburn is a jewel—this fringe area of the North York Moors National Park is in many respects as fine as the Cotswolds, albeit far less well known. The wealthier refugees from Teesside and the West Riding are however discovering its delights and the cottages have that artificial elegance nowadays which no labourer's wage can provide. Still, this is preferable to the slight feeling of decay that threatened only a short time ago. Observe in the village centre the half-timbered cottage of Robert Thompson—the great Kilburn woodcarver whose "mouse" symbol has become a legend for fine quality church and public building furniture. Thompson died in 1955 and his son and craftsmen carry on the expanding trade.

Enter the gate into the churchyard, climbing to the white gate beyond and a narrow tarmaced path up the hillside. This leads to the lane below High Kilburn (SE 516796), a pretty collection of cottages and a village green. Continue down hill along the narrow lane, and where it turns left go straight ahead down a green track crossing gates of wood and metal. Keep the same direction to a small barn, where turn sharp left and look for a gate in the pasture above you. This leads to a pretty, overgrown green way soon winding round to join the lane from Oldstead at Kilburn Thicket. Go right here past Fox Farm and where the lane bears right, a gate on the left by a tall ash marks the start of a path alongside a hedge.

Take the first gate on the right (530784), crossing the field to the bottom right hand corner and a fence-stile. Cross here to the field on your right, going back into the next field directly behind the first one (this is a shade awkward). Climb diagon-

47

ally here to another fence-stile in the top left hand corner, and keep alongside this field edge to the next crossing point. In a rather more open pasture, with the crenellated tower of Coxwold church ahead, bear left to a white kissing gate. A second gate beyond this marks your way, the church—where Sterne was vicar—now being well to the right. You emerge in Coxwold village at the *Fauconberg Arms*—a delight of this walk is the numerous ancient hostelries, suggesting a kind of sophisticated "pub-crawl." Coxwold is undoubtedly one of the finest villages in Yorkshire, having a noble parish church with an extraordinary octagonal tower, and several seventeenth and eighteenth century cottages and houses of great interest. A short way up the lane on the left is Shandy Hall, the centre-piece of *Tristram Shandy* and Sterne's home for a number of years. It was until recently sadly neglected, but the Laurence Sterne Trust has acquired the property and is restoring it as a small Sterne museum of Shandyana—a tribute to one of Yorkshire's most distinguished writers.

Take the Ampleforth road past the crossroads below the village and the ruins of Coxwold station. A white gate to the left (539770) marks the line of a path into Newburgh Park, but an alternative is to take the estate track above the lake. The house is a splendid Georgian mansion built in the grounds of an Augustinian Priory, and is reputedly the last resting place of Cromwell's bones. Follow the estate track which provides pleasant walking along the bottom of the Vale of Coxwold. After about two miles, shortly after crossing the old railway line, take the track marked by two stakes to Old Pilfit Farm (568772).

The next bit needs the courage of your convictions, although it is a public right-of-way. Go through the little gate to the right at the farm, and if the stile isn't yet replaced cross the low fence exactly opposite the corner of the farmhouse nearest to you. Climb up through the scrubby woodland—there is no trace of the path on the ground—and emerge at a huge field which is usually ploughed. The farm has a legal duty to replace the path, and you have a legal right to go straight ahead to the top corner of the crescent of woodland that curves round to your left. Keep the same direction to reach a gap in the top of the field; timid souls may prefer to follow the edge of the wood right round. Go through the obvious gap in the hedge, about a yard wide and then turn right to a gap in the next field on the right, going left alongside the hedge to a gate ahead (574777). You should now be alongside a tall hedge—follow it to your left. You soon pass an old wheeled shepherd's hut, exactly

48

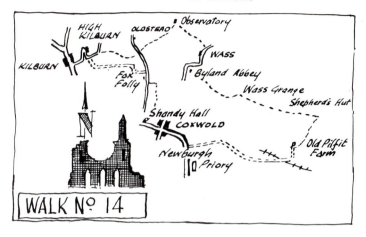

like that used by Gabriel Oak in *Far from the Madding Crowd.*
Make your way along the south side of a low wooded hill—
this is pleasant walking with good views along the vale. Take
care at an awkward corner, keeping the same direction and
crossing a low fence on the left. Another fence-stile ahead
joins a clearer way through a gate to Wass Grange farm
(563784).

Notice the tall hedge with a white gate to the left of the farm.
Follow this right round uphill and down, and then left towards
Craykeld Wood going through a gate to the right and then
alongside a wire fence. At the top of the next pasture cross the
fence-stile ahead, and turn left over a couple of rickety stiles
past the next two fields before climbing up to a little ruined
barn (554783) near Low Pasture House. There is a splendid,
view of Byland Abbey from here—make straight for the ruins
passing through a gate below and following a rather soggy
path through gateways. A gap on the left leads to a fence
going round the back of the abbey. Spend some time at the
massive ruin, noticing the remains of the huge cloister and
famous mosaic pavements.

Turn right at the cross roads by the *Abbey Inn,* but take the
first farm-track on the left towards a superbly kept farmhouse.
Before the farm go through the fieldgate on the right, climbing
the pasture to the left to a gate in the top corner. Bearing left
through more gateways to a track just above the hamlet of
Wass (553794)—also possessing an inn. You now take a
beautiful track left through tall deciduous woods. Where the

track bears sharp right go through the gate ahead on to an even lovelier green track—a steady beautiful climb soon totally enclosed in uniform trees. Where the track finally levels out and is joined by another on the left, stray off your route to enjoy superb views across the vale. The track soon bears left to a fine tower (537805), an observatory built to commemorate "the first year in the reign of Queen Victoria"—a gesture worthy of Tristram's Uncle Toby, as are the fine doggerel couplets on the blessings of Nature to be read by those energetic enough to jump on the stone plinth. The poet certainly had a point—here in the valley below you still exists the eighteenth century ideal, the balance of man and nature and a harmony which urban man has long since lost.

The gate just in front of the tower leads to a winding path. This is a "permissive" route; the Forestry Commission who own the land are tolerant of visitors who respect the woodlands and avoid all possible fire risk including smoking. The path joins a broad forestry track. Turn right before going downhill and soon bearing left into the road just above Oldstead, another of those delightful North Riding villages. There is a direct path from Oldstead back to Kilburn, but it is in a poorish state. I would recommend keeping to the Byland road though the village and going right at the *Black Swan Inn*. Just past a red pantiled farm turn right through a metal gate (528796). This unpromising muddy track is soon a pleasant and enclosed green lane. Keep straight ahead through gates to the pretty lane just above High Kilburn; this connoisseur's walk ends along the parishioners' way back to the church.

Maps: One Inch; Sheet 92; 2½ Inch Sheet SE57.
Sources: *Students of Ampleforth College: Ampleforth Country* (1958/68).
      Nikolaus Pevsner: The North Riding (1966).

15: Eighteenth Century Transport

Around Gargrave—8 miles.

GARGRAVE, on the old Keighley-Kendal turnpike road, has still much of a flavour of an eighteenth century coaching town. It was also an important little inland port on the Leeds-Liverpool canal, connected by a specially built turnpike to the Duke of Devonshire's lead mines at Grassington. Though the canal brought industry and prosperity to Airedale in the eighteenth and nineteenth centuries, much of the old waterway still goes through countryside of surprisingly high quality and nowhere better than the stretch explored by this towpath walk west of Gargrave.

From the village centre make your way up West Street to the canal bridge (SD 931544), turning left onto the towpath and past the first series of locks. Note the cast-iron milestones indicating the mileage between Leeds and Liverpool. A British Waterways Board water and mooring point indicate the new significance of the canal as a Cruiseway for leisure boating and, in summer months an enormous variety of pleasure craft will be seen. The towpath itself is not a right of way, but the Waterways Board has indicated that it has no objection to well-behaved walkers using the path. The strip of quiet, image-reflecting water is a delight, winding by trees and under fine stone bridges. It soon curves under the old turnpike, now the A65 and beneath the former Midland Railway. The canal crosses the river Aire by a fine aqueduct at Holme Bridge, for a period of about 25 years the terminus of the canal until sufficient finance was raised to continue the work. The towpath soon twists out into the lane with a faded notice requesting boatmen to take their horses onto the road; but a few yards further along the lane another notice, with bland and unconscious irony, forbids horses the use of the towpath.

Take the gate back onto the towpath, passing a spectacular series of locks at Bank Newton. A little care is needed at the next bridge, No. 165 (913528); do not take the inviting stile ahead but curve back onto the lane, crossing the bridge to the lane and entering the towpath again on the left hand side.

Peaceful waterway scene as viewed from a barge on the Leeds and Liverpool canal near East Marton. (David Joy)

This enters an extremely beautiful section in open country, winding in an enormous double curve and showing the true "contour" nature of eighteenth century canal engineering which avoided the expense of difficult embankments at the cost of increased distance. Note the remaining tow-rope guides holding rollers to protect walls at the apex of sharp bends—at least one remains in working order, the wood still showing pressure marks of tow-ropes.

With the notable exception of a tall wireless mast, this landscape has changed little since the canal was built through the rolling glacial drumlins of the Aire Gap. It enters a lovely wooded gorge and soon reaches the extraordinary double-arch bridge under another ex-turnpike, the A59 carrying a roar of lorries to and from East Lancashire. The bridge now requires steel supports against the pounding. Keep to the canal for a few hundred yards, crossing at the next bridge to East Marton church (908507). Enter the churchyard through a green gate, continuing up the lane to the main road and turning right to the *Cross Keys Inn*. The way back to Gargrave is behind the inn along the Bank Newton lane, over the canal by Williamson Bridge and through a wood, turning right opposite a small tip (911513) onto the Pennine Way. Follow the sign and faint path over pasture to an enclosed way which descends to a stile. Above the gate ahead is a stile back into the lane. Continue to the next Pennine Way sign leaving the lane by a bend at a gate and stile (905517).

The next stretch needs a little care. Follow the direction of the sign down to a footbridge and stiles over Crickle Beck. The path now bears left following the general direction of the shallow valley, through a series of stiles or fence-stiles. Where the stream bears right, beyond the narrow copse to your left, go through a fieldgate ahead. Keep roughly the same north-easterly direction, climbing a low summit with Scalber Hill to the left and the white trig station on Butter Haw to the right (922530). There are splendid views of the long Craven hills from here, ridge beyond ridge, with the railway below left and Gargrave slightly to the right. Avoid the temptation to follow the wall away to the right to a little copse on the hilltop, but keep straight ahead to the left of a wooden fence towards a fieldgate. The track from Scalebar Farm meets the path from the left; follow the track downhill across the railway. The Pennine Way bears right here, but the easiest way back to the village is to continue until the track meets a lane. Turn right, finding the path to the left through the black fieldgate at the first pasture on your left. This leads to the riverside, a pretty spot which serves as Gargrave's village green. If you choose you can cross the sparkling river Aire by the stepping stones.

Maps: One Inch Sheet 95; 2½ Inch Sheet SD 95.
Sources: *Colin Speakman: Transport in Yorkshire (1969).*
            British Waterways Board: Cruising on the Leeds Liverpool Canal (1966).
            Ramblers' Association and Inland Waterways Association: Towpath Trod: Leeds to Skipton (1970).

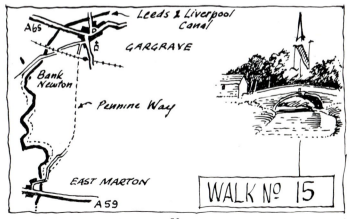

16: Eighteenth Century Highways

Marsden—6 miles.

M ARSDEN, at the head of the Colne Valley, is an unusual Pennine industrial town. For many years it was
an isolated outpost until the great road, canal and rail engineers
forced routes over or through the formidable Standedge in the
eighteenth and nineteenth centuries. They have left a distinct-
ive mark on the landscape. The town is reached easily enough
by bus, occasional train, or car along the main A62 Huddersfield to Manchester road. You may park near the parish church
(SE 047116).

Behind the church the infant Colne goes through the village.
Cross the little packhorse bridge, and make your way up the
steep muddy track behind the mill to your left towards the
railway station. Go left, before the station to a track by the
canal. An opening to the right gives access to the towpath of
the old Huddersfield Narrow Canal—an extraordinary piece
of canal engineering opened in 1811 at an expense of some
£300,000. The towpath follows a pretty stretch of the now
abandoned waterway, giving interesting views of the twin
Standedge railway tunnels to your left above the wall. Not far
past a fine old warehouse the towpath reaches a bridge. Cross
the canal here, but descend to the towpath on the opposite
side to approach the entrance to Marsden tunnel (040120).
At 644 feet altitude and 5,416 feet in length, it is the longest
and highest canal tunnel in Britain, representing a brilliant
engineering achievement by late eighteenth century standards
to drive through solid gritstone with only the simplest techniques of tunneling.

Climb to the lane on the right above the canal, going left at
the cross roads by the canal reservoir and cottages. Go straight
ahead at the next cross-roads and, at what seems to be the
entrance to an estate, look for an opening below and to the left
which leads to a bridle path on a causeway by the river. This
soon reaches Eastergate packhorse bridge (028121), a notably
fine structure. The bridge, deriving its name from one Esther
Schofield who kept a long-demolished packhorseman's inn

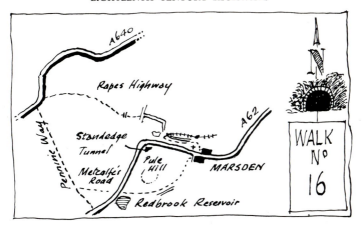

at this spot, is situated on Rapes Highway. An ancient packhorse road over the Pennine summit between Marsden, Old-
ham and Rochdale, the Highway was in use right up to the
early nineteenth century. It is also known as the Marsden
Packhorse Road or simply "th'owed gate." Even though this is
National Trust land, tractors laying pipelines have recently
obliterated part of the original road. Do not follow the paths
of the machines by the becks left or right; your way is due west-
nor-west straight up the steep nose of the hill that faces you.
As you scramble over the rocks reflect that laden packponies
once came this way. Soon a path is quite apparent, and there
are even traces of paving in places. It keeps straight ahead for
a few yards, before bearing right to cross a clough. You are
now on a wild stretch of moorland, to be avoided in snow or
mist.

The path bears north-west again, parallel to the beck with
the hump of Great Hill ahead as a rough bearing. Very com-
forting are fine granite posts, now mostly fallen, inscribed P.H.
Road and erected over 60 years ago by Saddleworth Council
to safeguard the disputed line of the road. Natural "pavements" of grit guide your footsteps as you climb, and on the
bleak summit of the moor the paler colour and slight rut in
the grass indicates the ancient road. This finally descends
quickly to the A640 and a beck behind a filthy laybye rubbish
tip, an unhappy sign of human pollution (004124). Don't
cross the beck but cut sharp left back along the Pennine Way,
a friendly turf cairn on the moor behind you marking the

routes. This is the great 270 mile walk between Edale and Scotland and it is almost certain during the summer months that you will meet some lone wayfarer en route for the Border. The cairns, recently erected by West Riding Ramblers, give desperately needed guidance over the waste and up the great black dome of Oldgate Moor.

Once over the summit, the path crosses a small beck (005113) and bears left to the craggy outcrop of Northern Rotcher. There are rather thrilling views across to industrial Lancashire as you make your way over stony outcrops on Millstone Edge and past the memorial stone to the West Riding poet Ammon Wrigley and the trig station (013104). Keep on past fallen walls; at the last of these, with the A62 and white Transport Cafe just below, bear left off the Pennine Way (105101) along a sheeptrack. Suddenly you are on Jack Metcalf's turnpike road. Blind Jack of Knaresborough, road engineer extraordinary, built this first coach road over the Pennines in 1759. It was an outstanding feat by any standards, especially when the engineer—surveying his route with his staff—was blind. This highway, broad and grass covered, is still quite discernible over the moor, although this section of it has been out of use for two centuries. Other parts are still in service. Sections of it were replaced in 1772 to ease the gradients.

Before the railway tunnel airshaft follow the path right along the top of a reservoir culvert to the main road (026100). Note the old *Great Western* coaching inn, commemorating Brunel's great ship, a few yards to your right. A path now parallels the Marsden side of the Redbrook reservoir ahead. It's easy to follow, but where it swings right round the reservoir leave it to keep straight ahead along the right of way bearing slightly left. This emerges on the metalled road a short way above a cross-roads; it is a narrow path and less easy to find. The road is of course Metcalfe's route. In the clough to your right are the remnants of the bridge that carries the 1771 road, still visible in the moorgrass. At the fork bear left, keeping left again up a quarry track above Metcalfe's road. There are pleasant views from here into Marsden. Do not follow the quarry road when it bears sharp left (043110) but keep straight ahead down the hill to an ancient green lane. Go through old gates, negotiated with a little care, to reach a farmhouse (045143), and follow the farm track, downhill almost to the centre of Marsden.

Maps: One Inch Sheet 102; 2½ *Inch Sheets SE*00, *SE*01.

17: Eighteenth Century Parkland

Castle Howard—6 miles.

IN 1699, John Vanbrugh, writer of brilliant if bawdy comedies persuaded the young Lord Carlisle to let him design a house. The result, which took a quarter of a century to complete and involved another architect of genius, Nicholas Hawksmoor, is Castle Howard. It is one of the great buildings of England, set in superb and carefully landscaped countryside that still illustrates the eighteenth century ideal of a balance between man and nature. This theme is highlighted around the great estate by the siting of splendid buildings and "follies" at strategic points in the landscape to produce an effect not unlike the landscapes of the painter Claude Lorraine. It may seem to jaded twentieth century tastes a shade artificial or even absurd, but it reflects an aristocratic vision of man's partnership with nature that we have some cause to envy.

This six mile walk captures something of this splendour for the landscape is little altered. Park in a quiet place in Welburn village, just off the main A64 York-Scarborough road, about six miles from Malton. Leeds-Scarborough buses pass the lane end, as do York-Malton local services.

Take the lane northwards which slopes away from the little green with a bench at the Malton end of the village (SE 722680). This passes Primrose Hill House on the right and is soon a track by arable land. At a gateway turn right by the fence along a track, which goes by a couple of wooden buildings, before bearing left above a small ravine into the well-named Pretty Wood. Keep bearing left up a narrower path through quite delightful woodland to reach an imposing monument "The Four Faces," a marvellous piece of neo-classical fantasy. Keep left along the track which follows the crest of a low ridge. Eventually, a track joins from the left, not far from a small wooden hut where are tall Scots Pines to your right. Your track now bears right, out of the woodland to emerge opposite a massive stone pyramid (723692) and a magnificent view of Nicholas Hawksmoor's great Mausoleum, tomb of the Earls of Carlisle and a unique and highly original building completed

The stately south front of Castle Howard, unquestionably one of Yorkshire's most imposing buildings. (Bertram Unne)

in 1733. It dominates the rest of this walk by its overpowering presence.

Keep straight ahead, crossing the farm track and making between fields for the ostentatious neo-classical bridge ahead. The Baroque dome of Castle Howard is just visible above the trees on your left. The fine bridge you cross was of course only built to improve the view, but it usefully carries the public right of way between the ornamental lakes. Above you to your left is Vanbrugh's Temple of the Four Winds, a summerhouse of delicate symmetry and proportion, described by one expert as one of the greatest small buildings of England. The interior was decorated by Vassali in the 1730s. This building, like the mausoleum, is strictly private. Descend the hill past the Temple, bearing left through a white gate to enter splendid mature oak woodlands. Keep right until the path meets the farm track from Coneysthorpe (722706), and then go right to Bog Hall Farm.

Just before the pantiled and brownstone farm, look for a gate on the left where the track bends past the big open barn (726708). This gate leads to a grassy track marked by field-gates with the white ruins of Easthorpe Hall on the hill above you. At the end of a narrow copse, just below the ground of the

58

derelict Hall, look right to see a gate. This leads to a bridle path skirting Spring Wood, a lovely green way through gates with fine views of the east face of the Mausoleum as you make your way across the springy turf. You reach a small farm where the stony farm track swings left, but your green way is to the right alongside a fence and woodland and through gates. It soon climbs a low hill and High Gaterley farm (739705) appears in the hollow to the right. Once under the telephone wires go right along the track to this farm, continuing to the next farm, Low Gaterley. Keep left below the buildings but turn right at the next junction near Pretty Wood. Go along the farm track close to the Mausoleum, past two rather incongruous modern houses dwarfed by the huge structure. Soon a unique view of Mausoleum, Temple, Castle Howard and Pyramid is presented before you, and you reach the track from Pretty Wood you had used previously.

If you wish to see the house you must continue along the track here to the gatehouse, the obelisk and the entrance. Opening times available from the Comptroller, Castle Howard, York. Otherwise take the track to the left by the Pyramid, keeping straight ahead past the Scots Pines. Bear right down the sloping track which crosses a tiny footbridge to return to Welburn. The church spire makes a most delightful bearing point ahead.

Maps: One Inch Sheet 92; 2½ Inch Sheet SE66, 67.
Sources: Nikolaus Pevsner: The North Riding (1966).
George Howard: Castle Howard Official Guide, (1958).

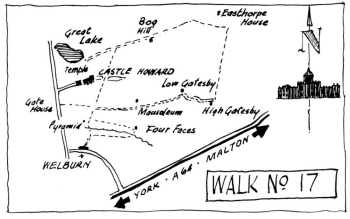

Bretton Park—5 or 9 miles.

BRETTON PARK contrasts sharply with Castle Howard, for it is situated on the edge of the Yorkshire coalfield near the woollen district. The industry that created the wealth to build the fine house and lay out the park and lake is very apparent, having grown since the eighteenth century out of all proportion. Whereas Castle Howard is still a home set in an aristocratic landscape and way of life, Bretton is surrounded by the strident industry of the nineteenth and twentieth centuries, and now serves the industrial towns in a way never envisaged by its builders—as a College of Education. The delight of this walk is this exciting contrast between rural and industrial.

Begin at Clayton West, a mining village easily reached from the M1 by taking the A636 Denby Dale road. Yorkshire Traction's Huddersfield-Barnsley buses serve the village, as does the single-track branch railway from Huddersfield which, at time of writing, still operates a useful weekday service to Clayton West. The station, reached by turning left in the village, provides an excellent car park and starting point for this walk. Take Back Lane, almost opposite, a dirt track by houses and a new factory. Go right at an obvious fork, keeping straight ahead as the track, transformed into a green lane, climbs to a gate leading into an arable field. Turn right in the field by the hedge, going left at the top to a stile. Cross here to a gate and stile ahead, turning left over it to reach Clayton Hall farm (SE270104). Pass the farm, keeping straight ahead where the farm track bends right—the path is on the left of the wooden fence—descending to a stile and concrete footbridge. Walk up the pasture to the stile ahead, turning left in the lane and crossing the stone stile to the right before the ruined cottage. Then climb up to the stile on the skyline ahead.

You are now in Bretton Park with its fine pasture and stately trees. This is a beautiful shaped landscape, with the infant river Dearne feeding two ornamental lakes amid trees. Beyond them is the College, originally an early eighteenth century house, enlarged in the nineteenth century and ex-

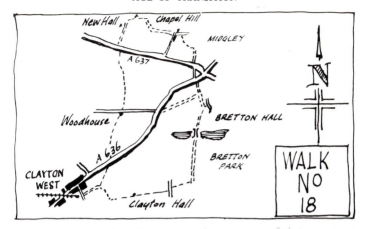

panded into a college in the twentieth century by buildings of unusually pleasing design. Keep ahead to a grass bridle track; turn left here, entering the woodland by ornamental gates and crossing the bridge between the lakes. Go straight ahead, but where the track bends right towards the orangery and into the college, keep ahead on the lesser track which soon joins the main drive from the college. Before the stone lodge (283132) turn left through a fieldgate along a faint green track and a scattered avenue of oak trees. This elevated path gives magnificent views back across the park and westwards to the grey summits of the Pennine ridges. Go through the iron gates at the edge of the park to a cross-roads of green ways. Those wishing for an easy afternoon stroll back to Clayton West, making a walk of about five miles in all, should turn left down a delightful green track going past woodland and emerging on the A636 road. Cross over, taking the Emley Lane for about half a mile uphill—the television mast is a dominant contemporary landmark ahead. Note the bellpits, probably for ironstone, on your right. From Woodhouse Farm (262131) follow the route described in the last paragraph of this section.

For a longer and delightful if slightly more difficult route, totalling about nine miles, keep straight ahead to the A636. Continue along the broad lane to the A637 and again go ahead along a green lane which enters Stocksmoor Nature Reserve. Pass through highly attractive woodland along a narrow and twisty path, keeping the same direction to a lane. Turn left here, going uphill to cross the B6117 and taking the road to the colliery opposite—a dramatic change of landscape with the massive red brick buildings and slag heaps dominating the woodland valley. Take care not to enter the works but, where the drive swings left, follow the narrow tarmac path branching straight ahead (274153). This soon becomes a delightful wooded way to the valley bottom—a narrow pitman's path climbing to Middlestown. But take the signposted path to the left (266162) to Chapel Hill; this is a beautifully maintained fieldpath. Note the conical slag heaps covered with scrubby woodland in every field, like tips of submerged volcanoes. Where the path, by now a track, meets a junction of many ways take the broad track left down to New Hall Farm. Keep left at the farm, outside the farm buildings, and pass through a gate leading between a duckpond and a wall—note the ancient oak sagging over the water. A stile ahead and to the right leads into the farm drive. The way suddenly descends into a little new housing estate, the homes of the staff of New Hall Prison just to your right. Assuming you will not wish to enter this detention centre, keep straight ahead towards a futuristic water tower on the skyline. Part way up the hill, look for a wooden stile on the left, which leads to a path over ploughed land emerging at a footpath sign in the field corner about 50 yards to the left of the water tower and on the A637. Cross the road, making straight for the farm ahead and to the right (264143) and going across more ploughed land before thankfully reaching a pasture leading to the farm. Ramblers who dislike trudging over ploughed land more than noisy roads should keep straight up the New Hall drive to the main road, turning right for half a mile to reach and descend the farm drive.

The path is round the far side of the farm, through gates and straight ahead down into Bank Wood—a steep hillside riddled with old bell pits dating from at least the seventeenth or eighteenth centuries. Keep slightly left between workings to a stile leading into a new plantation. With Woodhouse farm on the hilltop as a bearing, ahead and to the left, descend to the stream and find a stile leading to it. There is no footbridge over the beck (263137) which can easily be forded in all but the wettest weather (try further downstream in case of difficulty). Do not take the obvious stile ahead, but bear left over a second streamlet and then right to go up to the next field top to locate a stile. Cross here, keeping straight uphill to Woodhouse farm and stiles leading on the right of the farm to the road.

From Woodhouse go over the stile just to the left of the farm buildings, with a fence-stile behind it. Keep straight ahead downhill and behind the farm to a new fence-stile ahead and a series of sturdy wooden stiles. The second of these is hidden under a prickly hawthorn slightly to the right. Cross a concrete track at Gillcar Farm (261122), taking the stile ahead but keeping right alongside the hedge to a stile by a gate. Bear left here towards Clayton West and a little gate in the lane at the bottom corner of the field. Descend to the main road, crossing directly to the little packhorse bridge near an ancient house. The path is an enclosed way to your left, passing behind the factory football pitch and on to Back Lane. Turn right to the station.

Maps: One Inch Sheet 102; 2½ *Inch Sheet SE*21.
Sources: *Arthur Raistrick: The Making of the English Landscape: The West Riding* (1970).
       Nikolaus Pevsner: The Buildings of England: The West Riding (1959).

South Yorkshire has many oases of beauty among its industry. Examples are Bretton Park, described in this walk, and Heptonstall church, the tower of which is shown in this view. (see walk No. 20) (S. Outram)

The Nineteenth Century

Merryfield Glen—11 miles.

IN Ripley Castle, near Harrogate, there is a pig of lead discovered in 1735 at Hayshaw Bank, Nidderdale, and cast in 81AD in the Roman province of Brigantia. Lead-mining in the Dales continued right up to the present century, reaching its peak in the late eighteenth and early nineteenth centuries. This 11-mile walk explores the country where that industry took place; the intervening years have softened the industrial scars and given the area a sense of solitude and melancholy isolation, although at present there are threats that mining activity could return. It is fine rambling country, but as in all mining areas in the Dales potentially hazardous. Keep to the tracks at all times, and avoid the area in snow or mist. Above all, do not attempt without proper supervision and equipment to explore old workings or buildings.

From the centre of Pateley Bridge take the Harrogate road, turning left up the tarmac path marked Panorama Walk. This climbs steeply, but just past the cemetery take the narrow green ginnel to the left that leads to the little ruined church of St. Mary (SE 16455). The ruin merits a few moments' pause and exploration. Your path continues from a little wicket gate in the churchyard wall on the right, bearing slightly left across pasture and giving fine views over Pateley before reaching the tarmac path again. Pause at a little viewpoint on the right, and at Knott (168652) turn sharp left past the house to reach a grassy lane climbing upwards to a road. Go left here to the junction, finding a stile just to the right of the signpost ahead and then picking your way through gorsey banks to locate a second stile in the wall corner below. Keep straight ahead along the track which forms a spectacular high level walk, passing in front of the first cottage and then behind a house to enter Scot Ash quarries—a huge area of scooped out grit from which much of Harrogate and Pateley have been built (160666). Take care not to wander off the track, which soon thins to a path going straight ahead over spoil heaps rapidly being reclaimed by grass and heather. It eventually reaches a couple of stone stiles by gates into Wath Lane. Recently tarmacadamed, this lane is still quiet enough and offers excellent views up the dale and across Gouthwaite reservoir. Pass the cross-roads, but take a tiny green track right just above Pie Green Gill which cuts off a corner by gardens—this is public so go through the garden gate.

At the lane (149678) turn right, but just past the chapel take the stile to the left and cross the fields to reach the old Nidderdale Light Railway line. This was built by Bradford Corporation when constructing Angram and Scar House reservoirs and operated passenger services until the 1920s—look carefully at the house across the back and notice the platforms of the old station near the garage. Cross Wath bridge and take the stile directly opposite, climbing up wooden steps and past farm buildings. At first the route is straight ahead, but then bears left below a copse to reach a track by Spring Hill Farm (141673) and the lane to Heathfield to the right. Go first left, but before the old school observe the grassy ridge curving up the field on the left—this is the flue of the old Heathfield lead smelting mill. Follow the track round, climbing up the little ridge. Do not bear right into Highfield Farm, but continue straight ahead through the gate on the left giving access to a field path. The hedge is to your right, and soon a barn is to your left. Bear right over to Spring House Farm (138665); the path goes between house and barn and through the gate on the right to drop downhill into Merryfield Glen.

You are now on the old miner's track. At first the presence of numerous caravans detracts from the beauty of the valley,

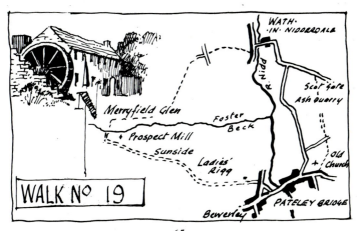

WALK No 19

but these are soon left behind as the route enters a fine wooded dale with a foaming beck below. Be sure to keep to the left where the track forks. As one climbs through gates the bracken and the heather moors close in, and the first sign of the old workings are evident—some little more than grassy scree, others still raw shale heaps. A large mess of spoil indicates the ruin of Prosperous Mill, a major lead smelting mill which, according to Clough, last saw active service about 1872. It once had a 14-foot "overshot" waterwheel for providing power to crash the ores. The flue is still visible running up the hillside to the ruins of a condenser built to dispose of the highly toxic fumes. The track soon passes several old "levels" or shafts into the hillside—do not enter these—and finally peters out around old workings. Follow the beck by a mixture of sheep track and path to a couple of small waterfalls and deep pools by a superb overhanging rowan. Past the last of the falls, just before a fence over the beck (109661), ford the water and follow a sheep track up the side of Gill Dike for a few yards. This leads to a green track running parallel to the hillside from a gate on the right. Take this way, going left and back down the valley. Should the beck be in spate and impassable , it might be necessary to cross at the footbridge (119662) and climb up to join the path from there.

At a fork take the track to the left in front of the wall. It gives fine views along the valley and passes more old workings before becoming more clearly defined behind Sunside Hill. After crossing Brandstone Dub Bridge (125655) the route is a broad track, curving round a steep little corner at a farm near Round Hill and then climbing straight over Ladies' Rigg. The isolated farm on the right is Bale Bank, its name indicating an early "Bayle" or primitive smelt mill. Keep straight on past Riggs House Farm. Where a pine wood on the right reaches the track, look for a rather hidden wooden stile in the corner of the field opposite (147654). This leads to a lovely path behind Eagle Hall, dropping pleasantly into Pateley opposite the Congregation Church at Bridgehouse Gate.

Maps: One Inch Sheet 91; 2½ *Inch Sheet SE*16.
Sources: *Robert T. Clough: The Lead Smelting Mills of the Yorkshire Dales* (1962).
Pateley Bridge WEA Class (*ed Jennings*) *Nidderdale* (1967).

20: *The Industrial Revolution*

Hebden Bridge—7 miles.

HEBDEN BRIDGE is one of the most fascinating and atmospheric towns in the Pennines, built on several small tributaries of the Calder—each of great beauty and character—which contained the birth of the Industrial Revolution from monastic times onwards. But it is the early nineteenth century that seems most evocatively captured in Upper Calderdale, in the narrow four-storey houses clinging to the hillsides, the zig-zagging "footstreets," steps and alleyways, and the mills hidden among the birch and oak.

Reach Hebden Bridge by diesel train, bus or car; there is suitable car parking at the railway station at the Halifax end of the town. Walk through the little park entered off the station drive by the gasometer. Cross the second bridge to the right over the canal; this is not the newer concrete bridge but the older stone structure that leads onto the towpath of Sir John Rennie's great but ill-fated Rochdale canal. Go over the aqueduct above the river, passing the mills, warehouses and confluence with Hebden Water on the right. Turn right before the next bridge (SD 988827) which culverts the waterway, going past the *Neptune Inn* and into the main street. Go left here, noting the zig-zagging paths ahead between houses and pass the Heptonstall cross-roads. Just before Greenbanks's timber yard (986273) take the enclosed path to the right that climbs above the mill hamlet of Mytholm. Go behind the church, school and mill pond, bearing right at a little fork between old gate posts. Keep along this route, ignoring paths bearing off to the left. Above a row of red-brick houses (982280) the path reverses back, climbing steeply and diagonally up the hillside and eventually up steps to a huge slab of grit. This is a kind of geological Pisa, a superb viewpoint through the great dark Calder Gap which is one of the most impressive gorges through the Pennines and on a cold misty day quite unforgettable.

Leave by the steps on the left of the rock face and follow a wire safety fence to the top of grit crags just below Heptonstall.

67

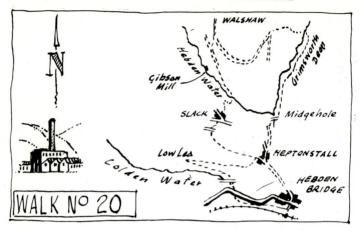

Unless you want to explore this fascinating village, do not take the enclosed path ahead but keep left along a high level and rather spectacular path along the valley top between the woods and the wall. At the pylons keep left, winding your way over the rocks just below the wall and finally entering a narrow lane to the right by a stile (979284). Fork right along the first green way you will see, climbing to an important junction of paths and packhorse ways—note the intriguing paved way descending to remote mills half hidden in the trees by Colden Water. Turn right up the broad green way to the hamlet of Slack (977287) with its huge chapel and ancient finger post. This is the old Burnley-Halifax packhorseway, marked for much of its way by the famous "long causeway" and ancient crosses.

Turn left at the cottage named Waterloo House and go down a path which soon enters the superb and dramatic gorge of Hardcastle Crags—known with some justification as "little Switzerland" and a magnificent National Trust property. The path winds past an isolated Jacobean farmhouse, now a Scout base, to stepping stones over Hebden Water. Turn left across the river by Scots pines to Gibson Mill, a fine but partially derelict watermill (973298) with a great millrace. Refreshment is available at the cottages during the summer. Keep to the main track, going up through the wooded reaches of Hardcastle Crags itself and bearing right with the main track to Walshaw. As you climb reflect on the fact that the recent Bill to flood the whole top section of the superb valley on your left was only narrowly defeated in the House of Commons.

On emerging from the wood (975310), turn sharp right along a high bridle road with good views across the surrounding hills. Pass Shackleton Farm and descend into Grimsworth Dean. One can shorten the walk by turning right here (987299), but for a more unusual way turn left and find a bridle path (986301) going into the next wood on the right. Fork right in the wood alongside the wall, descending to a mill pond. Negotiate the bottom edge of this with care, crossing a grassy bridge and going along an exciting little mill race with the gorge of Grimsworth Dean Beck well below you. At one point it is necessary to descend from the dike wall to cross a stream that breaches it, but otherwise it is fascinating and easy walking by a series of reservoirs that must have served the mill at Midgehole. At the last of these, indicated by a brick sluice and steps, do not climb the steps but descend to follow the fence down the gorge. Go through a gate on to a fairly well-defined green path and behind an asbestos shack into a green lane to Midgehole, passing right into the hamlet. At Midgehole (988291) cross the river, turning left by the Working Men's Club and keeping to the broad stony track that climbs the hillside. At an intersecting track (990288) turn left alongside a wall and on to the main road.

Several paths leave the road to the left to provide quite exciting descents into Hebden Bridge, but for the most re-markable of all stay on the road for about 400 yards past the 30 m.p.h. and the road junction signs. Turn left down an ancient cobbled lane, hideously steep and splendid above Hebden's mills and rooftops, and dropping to the very centre of the old town at the original seventeenth century hump-back bridge over the river. Turn right to the traffic lights; straight ahead is the park. Go over the concrete canal bridge and onto the railway station for train or car.

Maps: One Inch Sheet 95; 2½ Inch Sheet SD92.
Sources: Arthur Raistrick: Green Tracks on the Pennines.
      (1962).

21:   *The Industrial Revolution*

Haworth—8 or 10 miles.

IT would be inconceivable to have a book describing historic Yorkshire which did not include Haworth. Those three quiet Victorian parson's daughters, have indeed given Yorkshire international fame, and one of them, Emily, achieved the rare distinction not only of creating one of Europe's greatest masterpieces but of metamorphosing her environment to a universal poetic symbol. Little wonder that environment has caught the popular imagination in such an extraordinary way. Haworth remains, underneath the froth of souvenir shops and cafes, a typical West Yorkshire industrial village—Victorian in essence and clinging for existence to the inhospitable moors. Recently the branch railway between Keighley and Oxenhope has been re-opened by a preservation society, and the return of steam has added a splendid new period flavour to the valley. This walk then, for the newcomer to Yorkshire, revisits the usual Brontë shrines but does so in a less usual way and emphasises the other Haworth.

One might use the railway right up to Oxenhope—if the train isn't running visit the fascinating railway museum at Haworth station and walk on to Oxenhope. A very attractive route is reached by taking Sun Street, the continuation of Main Street, out of the village. About half a mile along the lane, after it has turned right and uphill a little, take either the second stile or the first track to the left (SE 033361) to reach a green lane down below a converted farmhouse. This descends through a wood and under the railway to a splendid packhorse bridge. Continue by the river side, across the next footbridge, but keep by the wall side below the farm to the farm track. Do not cross the river by this track, but go through a kissing gate on the same side to the next footbridge below Oxenhope station. Pass along the river bank to Oxenhope by a mill near the station, where turn right at the cross-roads and head back towards Haworth. Climb Moorhouses Lane, going left near the top at the postbox by an old farm. There are splendid views over the old town of Oxenhope to your left.

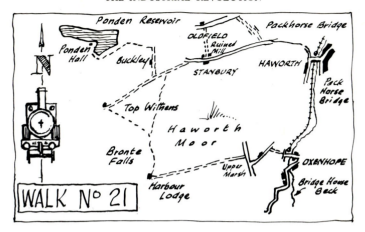

At Marsh (023362) turn left in the lane and then right along the edge of a roadside dump to pick up the path to Upper Marsh. You can work your way by quarry and moor ahead, but it is easier to turn left along the lane, right at the crossroads then left (018361) at the second track by the Craven Water Board sign to Harbour Lodge. There is no right of way along this track, but these moors have full legal right of access and you cannot be turned off. On the other hand, during grouse nesting and shooting it is only fair to be considerate and keep as much as possible to defined paths. This is a fine moorland track, but just before the gate into the lodge strike across the moor along a tiny and just visible footpath crossing sikes by footbridges. Keep alongside the stream on smaller paths, descending carefully to emerge at a popular and beautiful spot—the so-called Brontë falls which were a favourite place of the sisters. Across the footbridge there is a choice of ways. To your left a very well defined footpath climbs to the little ruined farm of Withens, allegedly the site of Wuthering Heights if not quite the building (SD 983356). It is a grim reminder of the harsh economic forces driving hillfarmers out of the lonelier Pennine moorland, and the change gradually taking over the landscape. Ponden Hall, supposedly Thrushcross Grange, is a splendid building of character. It is reached by following the Pennine Way along the top path from High Withins, via Master Stones and Upper Heights Farm and turning left down a broad green lane to Buckley and Rush Isles farms. Then go along the track to the left to Ponden (991371) by Ponden reservoir. Retrace your steps back to Rush Isles and

71

continue on to Stanbury. The more direct route to Stanbury for the weary or the blasé is to bear right above Brontë falls, passing behind the first ruined farm and above the second to join a sandy track leading directly to the village.

In Stanbury take the back lane behind the village. Look for a green lane beginning between garages from the Ponden end (008372) and dropping downhill over pavingstones, with a watercourse running over the path, to the gaunt shell of Griffe Mill. Go left round the mill to the beck, directly behind the ruin is a green bridge over the river Worth. Cross stile and wire fence to a winding green lane climbing up to Oldfield (SE 006378), a hamlet with fine eighteenth century and early Victorian farms. Turn right once in the lane, past the telephone kiosk and West House Farm to turn right into the next sunken farm track (014381). Fork left towards the lower farm, but don't enter the farmyard—go through a gate ahead and through pasture at a second gate. Where a farmer has fenced the way, follow the fence round to go through a metal gate to the right, and bear left. Cross a bridge over the beck going down to the valley bottom and a beautiful packhorse bridge (020375) over the Worth. Another green lane, a little muddy and overgrown, climbs past a derelict farm. Go up the track to the Stanbury road, turning left past the cross roads. At the large wooden sign, finish your ramble and this little book on what must be the most famous footpath in the whole of Yorkshire—the paved way, so often used by those reflective sisters, to Haworth parsonage.

Maps: One Inch Sheets 95, 95, 2½ Inches sheets SD93, SE03.
Sources: W. R. Mitchell: Haworth and the Bronte Country (1969).
R. T. Povey: History of the Worth Valley Railway (1963).
Arthur Raistrick: The Making of the English Landscape. (1970).
Joseph Craven: Stanbury, A Bronte Moorland Village. (1907).